A SPORTS ILLUSTRATED PUBLICATION

GOLF®

MAGAZINE'S

BIG BOOK OF BASICS

© 2012 Time Home Entertainment Inc.

Published by Time Home
Entertainment Inc.
135 West 50th Street
New York, New York 10020

ISBN 10: 1-61893-007-9
ISBN 13: 978-1-61893-007-1
Library of Congress Number: 2012941216

We welcome your comments and
suggestions about Time Home
Entertainment Inc. Books.
Please write to us at:
Time Home Entertainment Inc. Books
Attention: Book Editors, P.O. Box 11016
Des Moines, IA 50336-1016

If you would like to order any of our
hardcover Collector's Edition books,
please call us at: (800) 327-6388.
(Monday through Friday,
7 a.m.–8 p.m. central time or Saturday,
7 a.m.–6 p.m. central time).

Cover/book design: Paul Ewen
Cover/book photography: Schecter Lee,
Angus Murray

A SPORTS ILLUSTRATED PUBLICATION

GOLF®
MAGAZINE'S
BIG BOOK OF BASICS

Your step-by-step guide to building a complete
and reliable game from the ground up

WITH THE TOP 100 TEACHERS IN AMERICA

GOLF MAGAZINE
TOP 100 TEACHERS IN AMERICA

Edited by David DeNunzio

Time
HOME ENTERTAINMENT

Sports Illustrated

YOUR GUIDE TO
THE BASICS YOU NEED

Page-by-page, chapter-by-chapter, step-by-step: the fundamentals you need to improve every aspect of your game in the fastest way possible.

MEET THE PROS:
GOLF MAGAZINE'S BASICS TEAM

Your guides on the road to improvement—or any kind of game at all—represent the cream of the Top 100 crop with new insight to help you build the basics you need

THE TOP 100 TEACHERS IN AMERICA

Golf Magazine's *ranking is the definitive list of teaching talent in the country. Check the full roster on page 222.*

"THIS BOOK IS THE ULTIMATE GOLF PRIMER, WITH THE PROVEN BASICS EVERY PLAYER NEEDS."

JASON CARBONE, PGA

MIKE DAVIS, PGA

DOM DiJULIA, PGA

The book you're holding in your hands—*Golf Magazine's Big Book of Basics*—has been a long time in coming. Officially, it's the ninth entry in our popular line of instruction manuals, but the idea for it started years ago at a meeting among our Top 100 Teachers, who unanimously agreed that the majority of amateurs had lost touch with the fundamental skills needed to play the game well. According to these instructors, the general golfing public was focusing too hard on well-publicized theories that, in reality, meant more to highly skilled players than to the millions of avid golfers still treading water with double-digit handicaps. We, too, fell prey to the hype—many of our previous titles covered advanced moves and techniques. This one, however, hits the mark.

This book is the ultimate golf primer, with the proven basics every player needs to shoot lower scores. It doesn't matter if you're new to the game, frustrated with your ability to score or simply in the market for a refresher on tried-and-true mechanics, *Golf Magazine's Big Book of Basics* has it all. It covers everything there is to know about your setup, swing, mental outlook and even how to be a better playing partner or successful competitor. No more surprises. No more blow ups. Our Basics Team (*below*) has left nothing to chance, providing the direction you've been searching for to elevate your game to a whole new level. Enjoy.

David DeNunzio
Instruction Editor, *Golf Magazine*

BRIAN MANZELLA, PGA   LOU GUZZI, PGA   MIKE PERPICH, PGA   KELLIE STENZEL, PGA, LPGA

WHAT TO DO BEFORE YOU SWING

How to nail your grip, stance, posture and aim and get your swing on the right track even before you start

PRE-SWING BASICS:
GRIP, ADDRESS & AIM

INSIDE
Three ways to learn the basics you need:

LESSONS
Tips and instruction to help you master fundamental moves and positions

CHECKPOINTS
Tests to see if you're keeping up or falling behind in your quest to build a better game

DRILLS
Practice tips and step-by-step exercises to make new moves second nature

The little things you do before you start your swing make all the difference in your shots and scores.

When we discussed how we'd start this book, we didn't have to think long—we'd start at the beginning. In the golf world this means taking a look at everything that leads up to the actual act of swinging a club. While technique, swing speed and contact are definitely critical factors in playing the game to the best of your abilities, they won't mean a thing if your grip, address and aim—you know, the little things—are off.

Golf is unique in that it's one of the few non-reactionary sports around. You're not waiting for a pitcher to hurl the baseball toward home plate, or a running back to bust through the offensive line. Nope, it's just you and that little white ball—*and it's just sitting there.* Everything that goes into each and every shot you hit depends on you and how you set

up. You start in a static position, so it's critical that your starting position is rock solid—you can't rely on your ability to spontaneously react to something or someone charging your way.

In this chapter you'll learn step-by-step how to build a solid address position and prepare yourself to make the best swing possible. We'll cover the grip first. Good swings go bad even before they start if your grip doesn't conform to a few tried-and-true fundamentals. Next up is your stance, inclusive of posture, ball position and alignment. The important thing about address is that nailing it sets you up to swing back and through on plane almost automatically. When I see a good swing, I almost always see solid pre-swing fundamentals.

We'll finish it off with aim and alignment. As you'll soon learn, you can have the greatest swing in the world and still suffer if you think you're aimed in one direction while your body and club say otherwise. The lessons here are quick and easy. With a little patience and practice, you'll master the little things and be well on your way to working on the bigger moves that follow.

"WHEN I SEE A GOOD SWING, I ALMOST ALWAYS SEE SOLID PRE-SWING FUNDAMENTALS."

YOUR PRE-SWING PILOT

GOLF
MAGAZINE
TOP 100
TEACHERS
IN AMERICA

LOU GUZZI
Lou Guzzi Golf Academy,
Talamore Country Club, Ambler, Pa.
Golf Magazine Top 100 Teacher (2011–present)
● 2003 & 2010 PGA Teacher of the Year
(Philadelphia Section)
● PGA National Instruction Committee
● Teaching since 1992
www.louguzzi.com

PART 1: HOW TO GET THE RIGHT GRIP

Use proven grip fundamentals instead of what feels comfortable to gain max control of the club. Otherwise, the club will control you.

Your grip is the only connection between you and your clubs, so it's important that you make it as solid as possible. Your grip is the lifeline of your swing—if it doesn't function properly, then neither will the rest of your motion. Most golfers pay very little attention to their grip when learning the game. Even those with experience tend to forget about it, which is a major reason why the bulk of the golfing public fails to improve and shoot the scores they're capable of.

I've shot some pretty good scores over the years, and a lot of the success I had and still enjoy is a result of learning the correct way to grip the club at a very early age. I remember my first lesson—it was almost all about the grip. I also remember thinking, "How am I ever going to make contact with the ball?" A fundamentally correct hold in the hands of a new or inexperienced golfer feels awful. Don't give in to comfort. **The steps I outline in the first part of this chapter will set your hands where they should be, and it may feel very strange at first.** Relax. You'll get more used to this new grip with each and every swing you make, and it will soon be second nature—but only if you stick with it.

START WITH YOUR LEFT HAND

Your glove hand is your control hand, since more of it is in contact with the grip. Setting it the right way on the handle is Step 1 on your path to the perfect hold.

Check the big picture at right and hold a club like I'm holding mine. As you do, notice how the back of your left hand faces the sky, as does the clubface. If you cup your wrist and flex your left hand back, the back of your left hand will point toward you and, as a result, so will the clubface. If you bow your left wrist forward, the back of your left hand and the clubface will point directly away from you. **Hopefully you're getting the point: your clubface goes where your left hand goes.**

I've been using this image to teach the grip for many years now. I first saw it in a video featuring golf legend Lee Trevino instructing a group of amateurs, which came to me courtesy of fellow *Golf Magazine* Top 100 Teacher Ted Sheftic. I use this image with my students because, as you'll find out later in this book, straight shots are more likely to happen when the clubface is pointing at your target as you make contact with the ball. This means the back of your left hand also must be facing the target. Every movement your glove hand makes influences the position of the clubface, which is the reason why we'll start your path to the perfect grip by setting your left hand first.

START HERE ➡➡
Hold the end of the grip with your right hand and set your left hand at the top of the handle as shown, fingers pointing straight down.

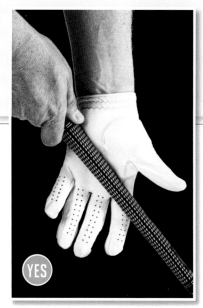

YES

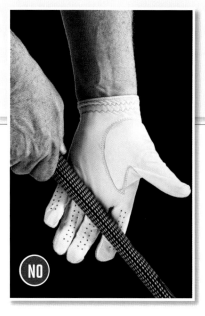

NO

PREFERRED LEFT-HAND POSITION

Using your right hand, guide the handle into your left so that it runs from the bottom of your left index finger through the soft pad below your pinkie. Next, wrap your fingers securely around the handle. You did it correctly if the grip sits in your palm *and* fingers instead of just in your fingers. This gives you the neutral left-hand hold most great players use. You can make adjustments as long as they don't move the handle out of your fingers and palm.

USE AT YOUR OWN RISK

This is the left-hand position most golfers end up playing with on the course, if only for the reason it feels more comfortable. As you can see, the handle runs across the base of the fingers. Using this kind of finger grip forces you to make compensations in your swing to produce straight shots. The bad thing about compensations is that they deprive you of rhythm, speed and power.

"YOUR GRIP IS THE ONLY CONNECTION BETWEEN YOU AND YOUR CLUBS."

CHART YOUR PROGRESS

Part 1: How to Get the Right Grip

- ☑ Correct left-hand position
- ☐ Ideal grip strength
- ☐ Correct right-hand position
- ☐ Connecting your hands
- ☐ Testing your hold
- ☐ Applying the right pressure

DIAL IN THE
CORRECT GRIP STRENGTH

How to decide if your grip should be neutral or strong.

Now that you realize how important your left hand is to the quality of your grip, it's time to choose how strong or weak you want that left-hand hold to be. I'm not talking about pressure here, just how much to the left or right you rotate your left hand on the grip. (We'll save pressure for later in this section.)

Like the dial on a stove, **the more you turn your hand to the right on the grip, the more heat (or strength) you'll get.** Some golfers need more strength, most often to get the clubface back to square at impact; others can swing perfectly well using a neutral grip. You'll need to experiment to find out which one works best with your swing. Eventually, your ball flight will determine your grip strength.

> "EVENTUALLY, YOUR BALL FLIGHT WILL DETERMINE YOUR GRIP STRENGTH."

NEUTRAL GRIP [LOW HEAT]
Only one knuckle visible, with the "V" formed by your left thumb and index finger pointing toward the right side of your chest.

CHART YOUR PROGRESS

Part 1: How to Get the Right Grip		
☑	Correct left-hand position
☑	Ideal grip strength
❑	Correct right-hand position
❑	Connecting your hands
❑	Testing your hold
❑	Applying the right pressure

WHICH GRIP IS RIGHT FOR YOU?

I always start out with a neutral grip. If I need more heat to get the ball flight I desire, I'll make it stronger, but I'll never go all the way to high heat. Never. That's me. You'll need to play around with the settings until you get the ball flight you want. Some guidelines:

IF YOU NEED THE BALL TO CURVE MORE TO THE LEFT: *Turn the heat up on your grip (left hand rotated more to the right), but never go full blast.*
IF YOU NEED THE BALL TO CURVE MORE TO THE RIGHT: *Turn down the heat on your grip (left hand rotated more to the left).*

STRONGER GRIP [MEDIUM HEAT]
Two knuckles visible, with the "V" formed by your left thumb and index finger pointing toward your right shoulder.

STRONGEST GRIP [HIGH HEAT]
Three knuckles visible, with the "V" formed by your left thumb and index finger pointing outside your right shoulder.

FINISH IT OFF WITH
YOUR RIGHT HAND

Create pressure points in the right spots by making your right hand a pistol before setting it on the handle.

There are two key things to keep in mind as you place your right hand on the grip: 1) Your hands should run close to parallel to each other once they're both set on the handle (i.e., Vs formed by your thumbs and forefingers pointing in the same direction), and 2) there are some areas in your hold that apply more pressure to the handle than others. Follow the steps here to nail your right hand position every time.

1 MAKE A TRIGGER
Point your right index finger out like a pistol, then curl it in while simultaneously pinching in your thumb. In other words, try to squeeze the upper knuckle on your right thumb against the bottom knuckle of your right index finger.

2 SET IT
Make sure there aren't any gaps between your right thumb and index finger as shown here. Keep those two fingers pinned together as you slide you right hand on top of your left and onto the grip. Set your thumb and index finger first before wrapping your right-hand fingers around the handle.

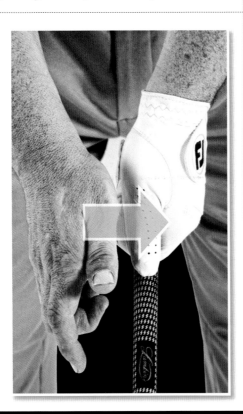

3 GRIP IT
Once you wrap your fingers around the handle, you should feel pressure against the thumb on your glove hand from the soft pad of your bare hand. You'll want to maintain this pressure from start to finish. Notice how my right thumb and index finger cradle the handle—I'm still pinching my right thumb against my right index finger. This cradling and pinching action is critical for securing the club at the top of your backswing.

CHECK IT!

If you set your right hand correctly using the steps at left, you'll notice that the grip sits more in the fingers of your right hand and a bit lower in your palm. That's good! Also notice that you're securing the grip with your right middle and ring fingers on the underside of the handle and with your right index finger (the "trigger") on the side. These are key pressure points (*see next page*). In fact, if you've done it correctly, then you should be able to hold the club out like this using just these fingers.

MIND YOUR GAP

A good grip has zero gaps. To make sure your right-hand hold is as solid as it can be, fold up a dollar bill and wedge it into the V formed by your thumb and index finger of your right hand. Make some practice swings (even if you're not yet sure on how to make a correct golf motion). Pinch the bill—it shouldn't fall out when you swing.

> "CONNECT YOUR HANDS IN A WAY THAT ENABLES THEM TO WORK AS A SINGLE UNIT."

CHART YOUR PROGRESS

Part 1:
How to
Get the
Right Grip

- ☑ Correct left-hand position
- ☑ Ideal grip strength
- ☑ Correct right-hand position
- ☐ Connecting your hands
- ☐ Testing your hold
- ☐ Applying the right pressure

THE FINE ART OF
CONNECTING YOUR HANDS

Interlock or overlap? Knowing the difference puts the finishing touches on your personal-best hold.

All grips may look the same at first glance, but closer inspection shows that each—yours, mine, your playing partners', Tiger's—is entirely unique. In fact, you'd be hard-pressed to find two that look exactly alike. Most of the idiosyncrasies you see the best players in the world build into their grips are long-standing quirks learned at an early age that, well, just plain stuck. Others are carefully calculated positions that the player uses to offset a certain swing deficiency.

You'll find examples of these differences on the underside of the grip, where you can choose one of three primary ways to connect your hands on the handle (*photos, right*). Like it was with grip strength, each option is as viable as the next. You have to experiment to find the right one for you.

No matter which style you choose, **it's important that you connect your hands in a way that enables them to work as a single unit.** This gives you the opportunity to exert total control over the club and create ample clubhead speed when you swing.

CHART YOUR PROGRESS

Part 1:
How to
Get the
Right Grip

- ☑ Correct left-hand position
- ☑ Ideal grip strength
- ☑ Correct right-hand position
- ☑ Connecting your hands
- ☐ Testing your hold
- ☐ Applying the right pressure

OPTION 1
BASEBALL GRIP

What It Does:
Creates max contact between your hands and the grip, with every digit touching the handle. As a result, it provides the greatest control.

How to Do It:
Set the pinkie on your right hand snugly against the index finger of your left hand.

You Know You Need It If:
You're a junior player, a raw beginner or a player with small or weak hands. Golfers who fall into any of these categories require as much control as possible until they advance or grow bigger.

Grip video lessons at **golf.com/basics**
and on the tablet editions of Golf Magazine

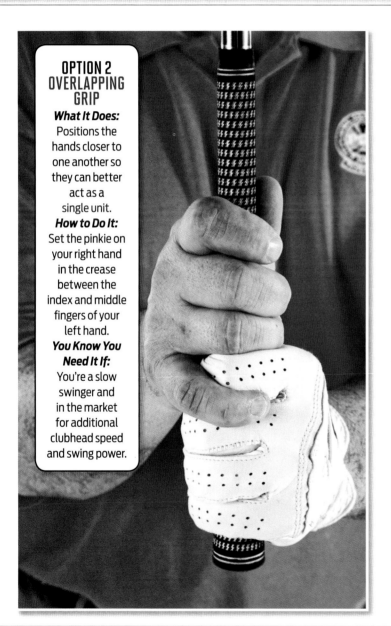

OPTION 2 OVERLAPPING GRIP

What It Does:
Positions the hands closer to one another so they can better act as a single unit.

How to Do It:
Set the pinkie on your right hand in the crease between the index and middle fingers of your left hand.

You Know You Need It If:
You're a slow swinger and in the market for additional clubhead speed and swing power.

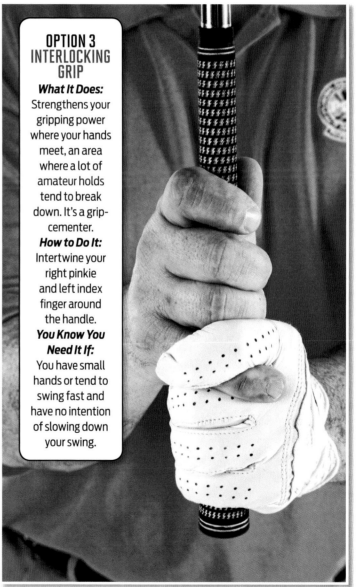

OPTION 3 INTERLOCKING GRIP

What It Does:
Strengthens your gripping power where your hands meet, an area where a lot of amateur holds tend to break down. It's a grip-cementer.

How to Do It:
Intertwine your right pinkie and left index finger around the handle.

You Know You Need It If:
You have small hands or tend to swing fast and have no intention of slowing down your swing.

HOW TO
TEST YOUR GRIP

If you've followed the steps thus far, you should be set. Here's how to see if you're on the right path or have made mistakes in your hold.

START
Repeat the steps from the previous pages, then settle into a solid stance as shown. (You won't need a ball for this test.) Next, bend you elbows slightly while hinging the club straight up with your wrists.

 YES

YOU PASSED THE TEST
If you can bring the club up so that the clubhead rises above your right shoulder as shown, congratulations! This motion should feel smooth, just like you're swinging an ax back when chopping wood.

 NO

YOU FAILED THE TEST
If your grip is off, then you won't be able to hinge the club up, at least without encountering some resistance. If you feel any interference at all, revisit the advice on the previous pages.

Q DO I NEED TO WEAR A GLOVE?

In my opinion, yes. Although you'll see some professionals play barehanded (Fred Couples has gone gloveless for 30-plus years), I think wearing one can only help. Gloves give you extra gripping power when you swing, helping the handle to stay in place. This is especially useful for your left hand because it leads your downswing, like a horse pulling a buggy. The pinkie and ring and middle fingers of your glove hand are really what secure the club as you swing down and to the finish.

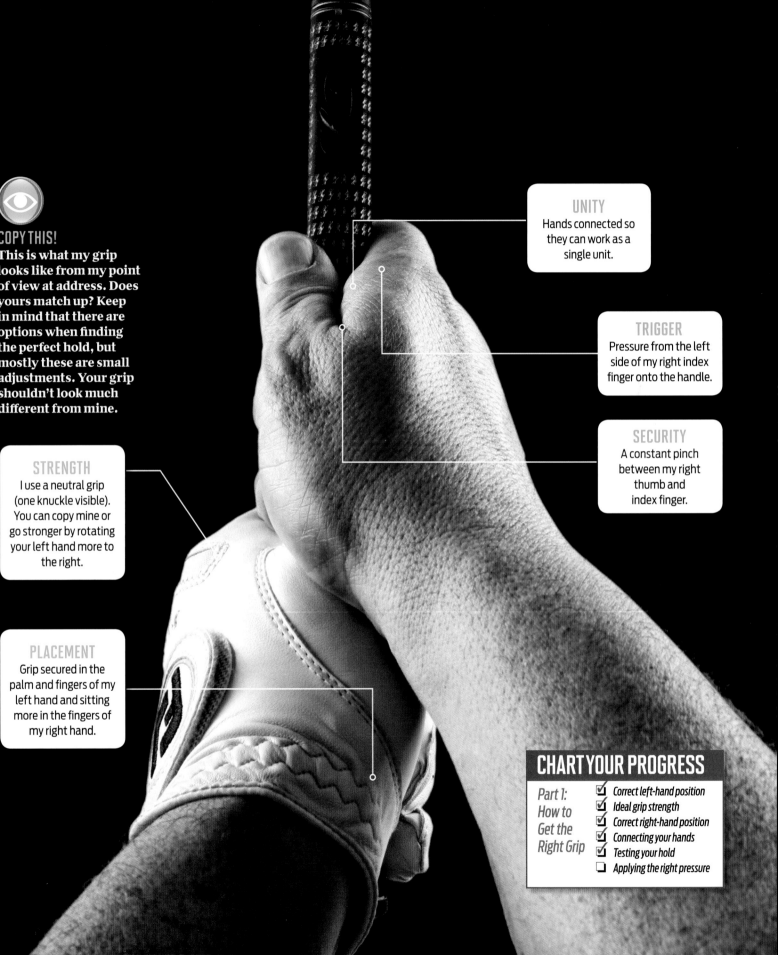

COPY THIS!
This is what my grip looks like from my point of view at address. Does yours match up? Keep in mind that there are options when finding the perfect hold, but mostly these are small adjustments. Your grip shouldn't look much different from mine.

UNITY
Hands connected so they can work as a single unit.

TRIGGER
Pressure from the left side of my right index finger onto the handle.

SECURITY
A constant pinch between my right thumb and index finger.

STRENGTH
I use a neutral grip (one knuckle visible). You can copy mine or go stronger by rotating your left hand more to the right.

PLACEMENT
Grip secured in the palm and fingers of my left hand and sitting more in the fingers of my right hand.

CHART YOUR PROGRESS

Part 1: How to Get the Right Grip
- ☑ Correct left-hand position
- ☑ Ideal grip strength
- ☑ Correct right-hand position
- ☑ Connecting your hands
- ☑ Testing your hold
- ☐ Applying the right pressure

CHECK YOUR
PRESSURE POINTS

The secret to securing your hold is applying force where you need it most.

Ask a dozen teachers how tightly, on a scale of 1 to 10, you should squeeze the handle on your clubs and six will say "8" and the other six will respond with "3." That's because grip pressure is relative to hand strength. Most Tour professionals use a light grip pressure (the 3), which they can get away with because of the tremendous strength they've built up in their hands and wrists over the years. (If you've ever shaken a PGA Tour player's hand, you know what I mean.) Most amateurs' hands aren't that strong, which explains the firmer recommendation.

The secret to nailing your grip pressure is to squeeze the handle just hard enough so that the club doesn't move around in your hands during your swing. Remember, keep your forearms and wrists relaxed so you can swing the club with maximum speed.

CHART YOUR PROGRESS

**Part 1:
How to
Get the
Right Grip**

☑ Correct left-hand position
☑ Ideal grip strength
☑ Correct right-hand position
☑ Connecting your hands
☑ Testing your hold
☑ Applying the right pressure

PRESSURE POINT
NO. 1
Wrap your left pinkie and ring and middle fingers firmly around the grip, pinching the handle into the crease at the bottom of your palm. Do it correctly and you should be able to hold the club out in front of you using just these three fingers.

PRESSURE POINT
NO. 2
With downward pressure, the lifeline on your right palm should fit snugly over your left thumb. If there's space between them, you'll suffer.

PRESSURE POINT
NO. 4
Notice how in a good grip your right palm faces the side of the grip. Apply pressure in this direction to activate your wrist hinge before you swing back.

PRESSURE POINT
NO. 5
If you see any space between the thumb and index finger on your right hand, pinch those digits together. Pressure there ensures a more connected grip and greater control.

PRESSURE POINT
NO. 3
Whether you use an overlapping or an interlocking grip, make sure that your right pinkie is applying pressure on your left hand, rather than simply resting on top of it. Just that little bit of pressure unifies your hands.

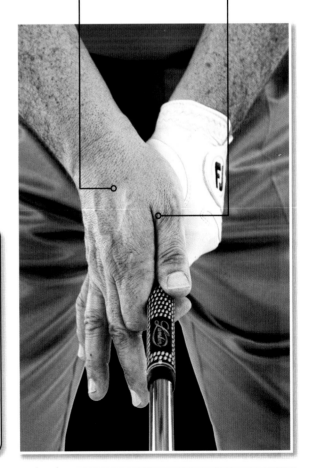

PART 2: HOW TO ADDRESS THE BALL

The way you stand over the ball defines the structure of your swing as well as its chance for failure or success. Here's how to get into your address position consistently and without error, focusing on the correct posture, ball position for the club you're using and aim.

PREVIEW
12 KEY ADDRESS POSITION NEEDS
Getting these right gives you an athletic, balanced stance you can use on every swing to hit the best shots possible.

When working on your address position, do it in front of a mirror and copy the positions that you see in the photos on these pages and the ones that follow. As the saying goes, "a picture is worth a thousand words." **Take in what your body feels like, but remember: this is only a guide.** There have been thousands of great players over the years, and no two setups have ever been perfect matches. That having been said, sticking to a few time-proven fundamentals will get you in position to start your swing on plane and increase your chances of hitting a successful shot.

1. SHOULDER TILT
Right shoulder slightly lower than your left (about the same distance your right hand sits lower than your left hand on the handle).

2. SPINE TILT
Away from the target, about 10 degrees.

3. STANCE WIDTH
Dictated by club length; longer clubs require wider stances. Notice that I've flared both feet for a more athloetic setup.

4. BALL POSITION
Dictated by club; play the ball forward in your stance with longer clubs.

Address position video lessons at **golf.com/basics**
and on the tablet editions of Golf Magazine

8. FORWARD BEND
About 25 degrees—
tilted from your hips.

9. HIP BEND
Tilted forward from
the hips so that your
belt buckle points
toward the ground.

10. ALIGNMENT
Body lines (shoulders,
hips, knees and toes)
pointed parallel left of
starting line.

11. KNEE FLEX
Just enough to feel
balanced and athletic.

12. DISTANCE FROM BALL
Dictated by club length; the
longer the club, the greater
the distance between you
and the ball.

"NO TWO SETUPS HAVE EVER BEEN PERFECT MATCHES."

7. ARM DISTANCE
Hands about two
fist widths from
your body for a free
arm swing.

5. WEIGHT DISTRIBUTION
Weight balanced evenly
over both feet (or slightly
favoring your right foot)
and set over the
balls of both feet.

6. SHAFT LEAN
Point the butt end of
the club at the inside
of your left thigh.

HOW TO CREATE
PERFECT POSTURE

Choose one of two ways to set your body in the most efficient hitting position.

When instructors talk about posture they're mostly concerned with three key areas of your address position: 1) forward bend (how far you tilt your upper body toward the ball, 2) knee flex and 3) arm and hand position. The most important factor is forward bend (aka, spine tilt)—if you stand too tall your swing will probably be too flat, and if you hunch too far over, your swing will probably be too upright. **Here are two ways to set your address position correctly (and to use as checkpoints if you start creeping back into bad habits).**

NOTES ON WEIGHT DISTRIBUTION
Whether you use method 1 or method 2, you should feel balanced and athletic at the end, with your weight in the middle of your stance and spread across the balls of both feet.

METHOD 1
FLEX, THEN BEND

STEP 1
Stand tall with the club out in front of you as shown. (Be sure to use the solid grip you built on the previous pages.) Set your biceps against both sides of your torso, with your elbows pointing toward the ground.

STEP 2
Without moving anything else, flex your knees slightly.

CHART YOUR PROGRESS
Part 2:
How to
Address
the Ball

☑ Posture
❑ Spine tilt
❑ Position checklist
❑ Ball position
❑ Aim and alignment

METHOD 2
BEND, THEN FLEX

STEP 1
Stand erect and set the shaft of the club against your body as shown.

STEP 2
Pull the clubshaft into your body—use the pressure to bend forward toward the ball from where the shaft hits. It should feel like you're pulling the shaft into the crease made in your pants as you bend forward. Stop bending when your chest is over your toes.

STEP 3
Bend your knees. Set the club down and allow your arms to dangle. They should hang straight down, with your hands far enough from your thighs that your arms have ample room to swing freely.

STEP 3
Without moving anything else, bend forward from your hips and keep bending until the club hits the ground. Your hands should be far enough from your thighs that your arms have plenty of room to swing freely back and through.

STEP 4
Step toward the ball without changing your posture to finish it off.

AN ADDRESS SECRET:
PINCH AND TILT

If you simply bend forward and flex your knees, you won't feel very athletic. Try these two moves to get into a swinging mindset from a static position.

f you followed the advice on the previous pages you've achieved a fairly solid address position without having to do much work. **But you probably feel a little restricted**. One reason for this is that you may be experiencing correct posture for the first time, and new feels can be awkward. A more likely reason is that your run-of-the-mill address sets you in a very static position—not good when your goal is to get the club moving upward of 80 to 100 miles per hour. Try the following to feel more athletic and "hit-ready" at setup.

CHART YOUR PROGRESS

Part 2:
How to
Address
the Ball

☑ Posture
☑ Spine tilt
☐ Position checklist
☐ Ball position
☐ Aim and alignment

GET SET
Use one of the methods on the previous two pages to settle into your address posture. Make sure your clubface is pointing down your starting line (*see page 34*) and that your shoulders, hips, knees and feet are set parallel to this line.

PINCH
Move your knees together as if you were trying to squeeze a beach ball between your legs. If you do it correctly, you'll feel your weight move to the inside of both thighs. Activating your leg muscles like this is good for your overall motion.

NOTES ON STANCE WIDTH

The width of your stance can vary a bit. A word of caution, however: the wider you make your stance the more you limit how much you can rotate during your swing, and the narrower you make your stance the more you risk losing your balance. Some guidelines:

LONGER CLUBS: Set the insides of both feet even with the outsides of both shoulders. This is the widest your stance should ever be.

SHORTER CLUBS: Set your feet directly under your hips. This is the narrowest your stance should ever be.

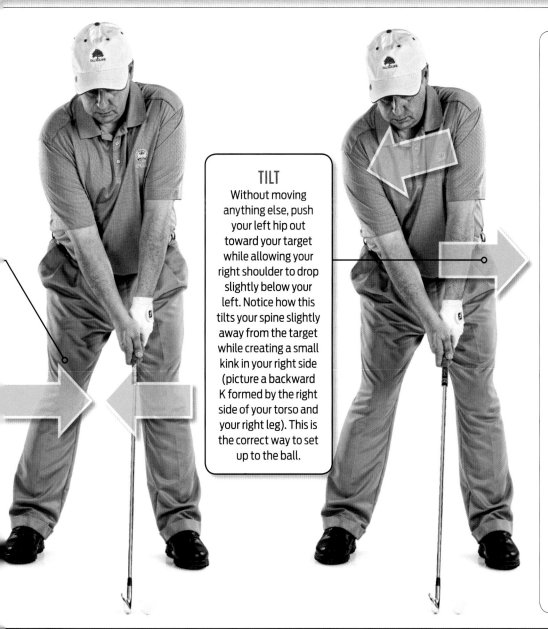

TILT

Without moving anything else, push your left hip out toward your target while allowing your right shoulder to drop slightly below your left. Notice how this tilts your spine slightly away from the target while creating a small kink in your right side (picture a backward K formed by the right side of your torso and your right leg). This is the correct way to set up to the ball.

FEEL THE TILT

When you push your left hip out and your right shoulder drops, the tilt is good because it matches how your right hand sits on the grip compared with your left. Here's how to determine how much tilt you need at address.

1 Stand in a mock address position without a club and clap your hands together.

2 Slide your right hand down until the upper knuckle on your left thumb is even with the lower knuckle of your right thumb, allowing your right shoulder to drop accordingly and your spine to tilt. Now, you're solid.

HOW TO CHECK IF
YOU'RE SETTING UP CORRECTLY

Nail these key positions to establish a fool-proof setup before working on the remaining parts of your address.

So far so good, but let's make sure you're exactly where you need to be and not skipping out on any important address-position details. **Again, use a mirror when gauging your progress. If the best players in the world do it, so can you.**

YES

FORWARD BEND CHECK

Get into your address position and dangle a club from your left shoulder. It should point to the toes on your left foot.

YES

ARM HANG CHECK

Get into your address position without a club and simply allow your arms to hang freely. Your hands should dangle just in front of your knees.

YES

KNEE FLEX CHECK

Hold a club straight up and down against your left knee. It should point to the ball of your left foot (or the laces on your shoe).

CHART YOUR PROGRESS

Part 2: How to Address the Ball

- ☑ Posture
- ☑ Spine tilt
- ☑ Position checklist
- ❑ Ball position
- ❑ Aim and alignment

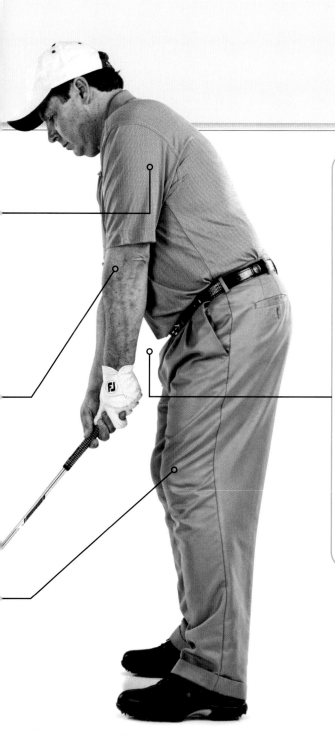

 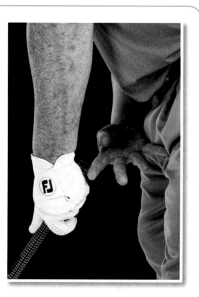

YES ARM DISTANCE CHECK

Get into your address position with any club, remove your right hand from the grip, and set it palm-up between the cap of the handle and your body. Your hands should be anywhere from a fingers-tight to a fingers-splayed distance from your trousers. If they're farther away from your body than this, you're standing too far from the ball. If they're closer, then you're crowding the ball.

 ### OTHER CHECKPOINTS
Don't forget these subtle—yet key—positions:
- Left arm straight
- Right arm bent slightly
- Elbows close together and pointing down
- Butt of the club points at the inside of your left thigh
- Knees pinched in

YOUR GUIDE TO
BALL POSITION

Take a lesson from Jack Nicklaus and Ben Hogan to set the ball in the right place in your stance every time.

One of the biggest problems I see with most amateurs is playing the ball too far back in the stance. This forces you to hang back on your right side through impact and stops you from correctly moving forward into a powerful finish.

The other problem I see is inconsistency: amateurs rarely set the ball in the same place twice with the same club. My advice is to keep your ball position constant. Follow the lead of Jack Nicklaus and Ben Hogan, who positioned the ball in the same spot relative to their left foot (even with the inside of the left foot for Nicklaus, and an inch behind the inside of the left foot for Hogan) on all standard full swings. Do this, then adjust the ball's position relative to your stance for the club in your hands by moving your right foot either closer or farther away from your left. The ball will appear to move back in your stance the closer you move your right foot to your left. Conversely, it will appear more forward in your stance the farther away you move your right foot from your left.

HERE'S THE PROPER SEQUENCE

1 Set your left heel opposite the ball. (Start here, but feel free to move it up to three inches ahead of the ball as you experiment.)

2 Position your right foot closer or farther away from your left foot (*see guidelines, right*) to automatically move the ball forward or back in your stance.

CHART YOUR PROGRESS

Part 2: How to Address the Ball	☑ Posture
	☑ Spine tilt
	☑ Position checklist
	☑ Ball position
	☐ Aim and alignment

DRIVER
BALL POSITION
Opposite left heel.
STANCE WIDTH
Widest (distance between outsides of shoulders equal to the distance between the insides of both shoes).
WEIGHT DISTRIBUTION (L/R)
45%/55%.

55%   45%

NOTES ON SHAFT LEAN

Keep it simple here. Regardless of which club you're using and where the ball sits relative to your stance, point the butt end of the grip at the inside of your left thigh. Doing this sets the shaft in a great position and leaning just slightly toward the target.

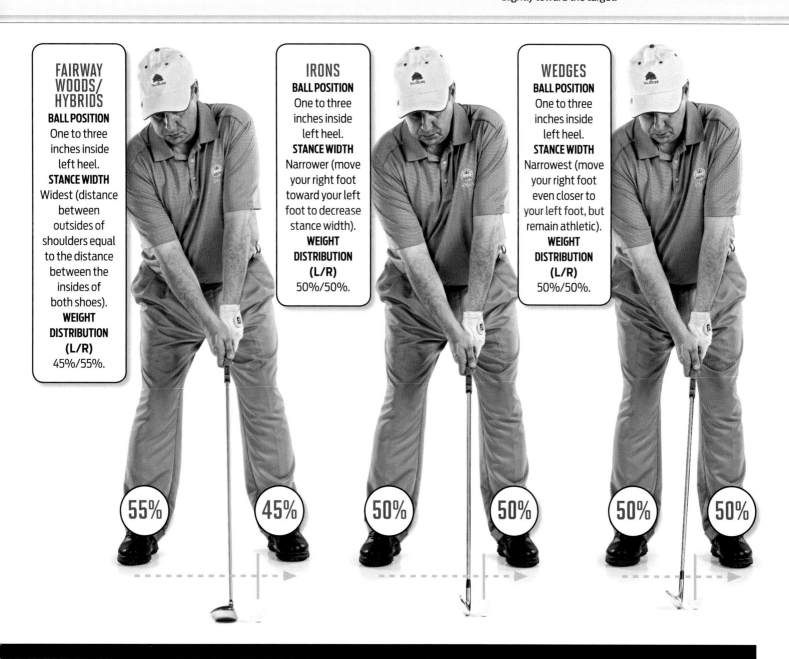

FAIRWAY WOODS/ HYBRIDS

BALL POSITION
One to three inches inside left heel.
STANCE WIDTH
Widest (distance between outsides of shoulders equal to the distance between the insides of both shoes).
WEIGHT DISTRIBUTION (L/R)
45%/55%.

IRONS

BALL POSITION
One to three inches inside left heel.
STANCE WIDTH
Narrower (move your right foot toward your left foot to decrease stance width).
WEIGHT DISTRIBUTION (L/R)
50%/50%.

WEDGES

BALL POSITION
One to three inches inside left heel.
STANCE WIDTH
Narrowest (move your right foot even closer to your left foot, but remain athletic).
WEIGHT DISTRIBUTION (L/R)
50%/50%.

55% 45% 50% 50% 50% 50%

HOW TO ALIGN AND
AIM AT YOUR TARGET

Hitting the ball in the direction you want is a game of parallel lines and targets.

There are three key terms you need to learn and understand before you can master alignment and play your best golf.

1. Starting Line The line on which you want the ball to start as it leaves the clubface.

2. Intermediate Target A spot in the fairway or on the green where you want the ball to land.

3. Destination Target Where you want the ball to end up after it hits your intermediate target.

Your goal at address is to point the clubface down the starting line and then set your feet, knees, hips and shoulders parallel to the starting line. For most players, this is the easiest way to make sure they're both aimed and aligned correctly.

HOW TO DO IT

When lining up, visualize a brick wall about three feet behind your back, pointing parallel left of your starting line. Everything—clubface, shoulders, hips, knees and feet—should be parallel to the wall. This is your set position. If the target is more to the left, turn the whole arrangement in that direction, like you're sitting atop a lazy Susan (*photos, right*). The same goes if the target is more to the right.

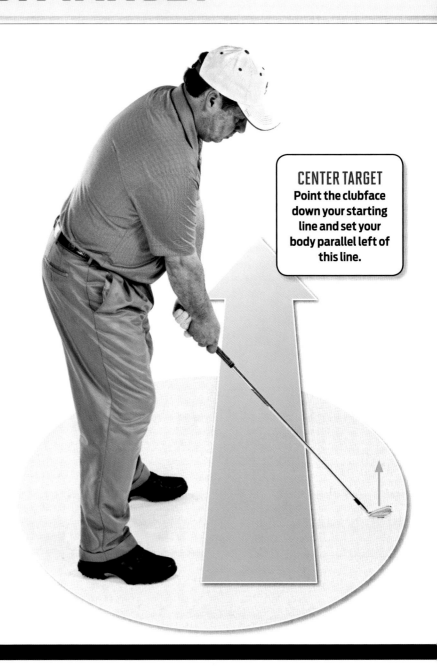

CENTER TARGET
Point the clubface down your starting line and set your body parallel left of this line.

NOTES ON TENSION

Most courses feature intimidating holes and shots, and focusing on their difficulty as you take your address and align to your target will only cause you to freeze up and keep you from performing at your maximum potential. **To combat the tension that comes from anxiety or fear over difficult shots,** **picture a goalpost on your target line or, if you intend to curve the ball, on your starting line.** *That should be the only thing on your mind—seeing the ball sail through the posts. This wider margin for error will help you relax and better visualize the shot you're trying to hit, which is always a benefit.*

RIGHT TARGET
Swivel the whole arrangement clockwise if the target is out to the right...

LEFT TARGET
...and counter-clockwise if the target is to the left.

HOW TO ACCOMMODATE
FADES AND DRAWS

Most golfers are born to curve the ball one way or the other. Here's the smart way to adjust your aim to take advantage of your natural fade or draw.

IF YOU TEND TO FADE THE BALL...
Aim to the left based on how much left-to-right curve you produce on your shots. For example, if you fade the ball 20 yards with your driver, then aim 20 yards to the left of your intermediate target on the tee box.

IF YOU TEND TO DRAW THE BALL...
Aim to the right based on how much right-to-left curve you produce on your shots. For example, if you draw the ball 20 yards with your driver, then aim 20 yards to the right of your intermediate target on the tee box.

The more you play the game, the more you'll come to realize that your everyday swing produces a consistent ball flight—a signature shot shape, if you will. Personally, I tend to produce a soft left-to-right (fade) curve with my longer clubs, and a mild right-to-left (draw) curve with my shorter irons. Instead of fighting your tendencies (once you establish them), the trick is to max them out by adjusting the aim-and-align principles discussed on the previous pages. That's when you'll start to hit more fairways and hit more greens in regulation.

CHART YOUR PROGRESS

Part 2:
How to
Address
the Ball

☑ Posture
☑ Spine tilt
☑ Position checklist
☑ Ball position
☑ Aim and alignment

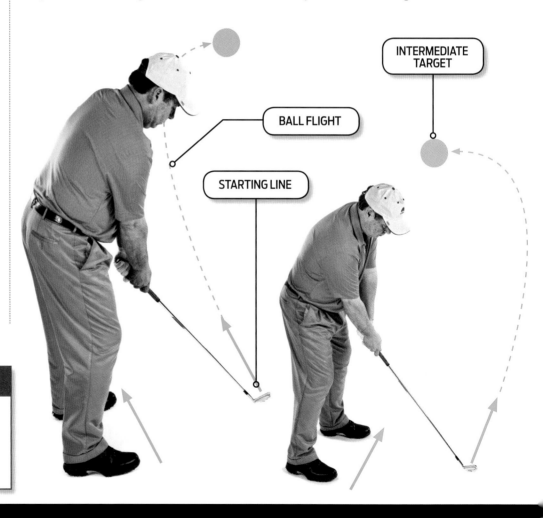

BALL FLIGHT

STARTING LINE

INTERMEDIATE TARGET

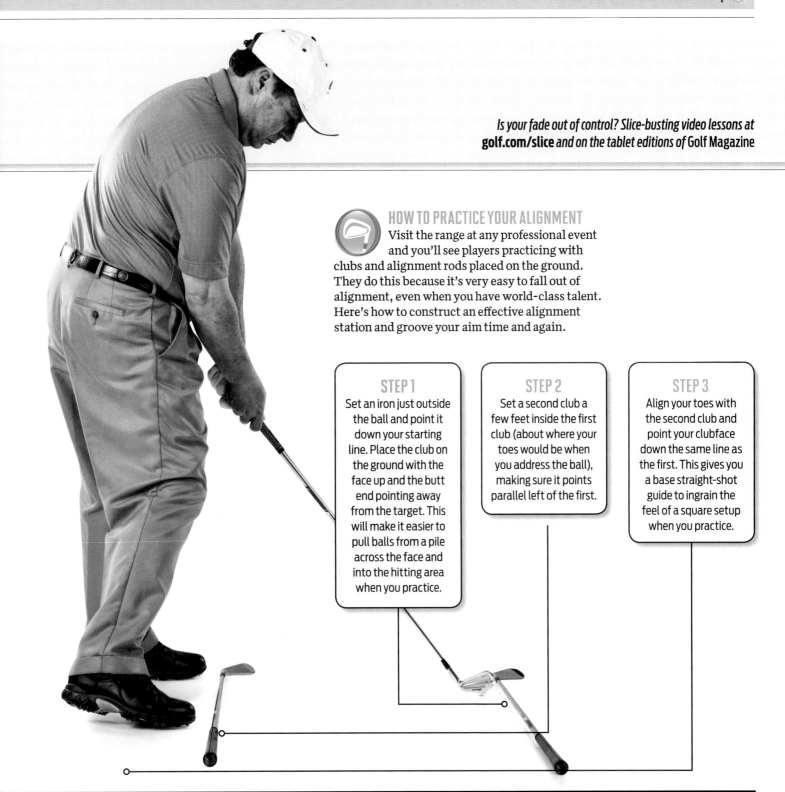

Is your fade out of control? Slice-busting video lessons at **golf.com/slice** *and on the tablet editions of* Golf Magazine

HOW TO PRACTICE YOUR ALIGNMENT

Visit the range at any professional event and you'll see players practicing with clubs and alignment rods placed on the ground. They do this because it's very easy to fall out of alignment, even when you have world-class talent. Here's how to construct an effective alignment station and groove your aim time and again.

STEP 1
Set an iron just outside the ball and point it down your starting line. Place the club on the ground with the face up and the butt end pointing away from the target. This will make it easier to pull balls from a pile across the face and into the hitting area when you practice.

STEP 2
Set a second club a few feet inside the first club (about where your toes would be when you address the ball), making sure it points parallel left of the first.

STEP 3
Align your toes with the second club and point your clubface down the same line as the first. This gives you a base straight-shot guide to ingrain the feel of a square setup when you practice.

PART 3:
YOUR PRE-SHOT ROUTINE

Golf is hardly a reaction sport, so finding a pre-shot routine that's repeatable and allows you to comfortably settle into your stance and then smoothly pull the trigger is absolutely critical.

Transitioning from approaching the ball to hitting it—including selecting a shot, pulling a club and finding a target—pulls all of the pieces of your pre-swing puzzle into a complete motion. There are probably a million different ways to transition into the act of swinging, but I'll share with you the one I use and teach my students. Give it a go and you'll quickly add your own elements to make it more personal and consistent. Regardless, use the same routine on each and every swing. Consistency may be boring, but it'll pay off in better shots and lower scores.

STAGE 1

Evaluate the shot you want to hit and select your club. Stand behind the ball and make a few practice swings. Your goal at this stage is to get a feel for the club in your hand. Remember, you may have just hit a driver off the tee and are now holding a 9-iron.

STAGE 2

Once you're comfortable with your practice swing(s), stand behind the ball and select your starting line. Bring it in with your eyes until you're focused on a spot about the size of a compact disc and about three feet in front of the ball sitting on your starting line.

STAGE 4

Settle into your stance while focusing on the ball, then look up and visualize a goalpost on your starting line, seeing the ball sail straight through the middle of it. As you do this, waggle the club back and forth to loosen up your forearms and wrists.

Waggle once.

STAGE 3

Start moving toward your setup position, bringing the club in behind the ball while continuing to stare at your compact-disc-sized spot on the ground. Once you've aimed the club through the middle of the disc, set your feet, knees, hips and shoulders parallel left of the starting line.

Use your imaginary spot on the ground in front of the ball to square the clubface to your starting line.

WORK WITH A MIRROR

The most effective way to work on your pre-swing fundamentals is to practice them in front of a mirror. Nothing is more powerful than giving yourself the opportunity to see what you're trying to accomplish. So far I've given you a lot of positions to focus on. The teachers who follow will do likewise. **A mirror provides you with an opportunity to self-teach and to instantly check if you're successfully mastering each and every lesson.** Look at the pictures, copy the positions in a mirror and take in what each position feels like. Mirror work is an integral part of improving, whether you're a beginner or the No. 1 golfer in the world.

Waggle again.

STAGE 5

As soon as you finish the second waggle, start your swing. Don't hesitate—the key is to create a smooth motion. The next time you watch a tournament on TV, track your favorite player and see if you can pick up on his or her pre-shot routine. Odds are you'll see it on each and every swing.

Pull the trigger.

HOW TO BUILD YOUR BASIC SWING

A step-by-step guide to blending the correct body and arm movements in each section of your swing for a smooth, powerful and consistent motion

STEP-BY-STEP:
A SWING YOU CAN TRUST

INSIDE
Three ways to learn the basics you need:

LESSONS
Tips and instruction to help you master fundamental moves and positions

CHECKPOINTS
Tests to see if you're keeping up or falling behind in your quest to build a better game

DRILLS
Practice tips and step-by-step exercises to make new moves second nature

The secret to learning any motor skill is to practice it in parts first and then pull the parts together. That's the way to build a swing you can trust for a lifetime.

Much has been written about the swing over the last century, including hundreds—if not thousands—of different ways to both think about it and put one in motion. The aim of this chapter isn't to applaud or debunk any of these methods, but rather to boil them down to the key ingredients all great motions share. Let's start with a definition.

YOUR SWING \yər 'swiŋ\ **n**: A controlled movement, powered by your body and arms working in unison, that motions the club on an angled circle around a central point.

Your golf swing is really as simple as that—you move the club back and through on an arc. The key is that you *swing the club*. You don't *hit a ball*. The moment you shift your focus from swinging to hitting is the moment you make the game the brutally difficult endeavor that ends up forcing both beginners and experienced players alike to lose interest and stop playing.

My goal on the following pages is to show you the body and arm movements that will get you into the proper swinging mindset. As you'll learn, executing these moves automatically positions the shaft, clubhead and clubface where they need to be in each section of your swing (*below*). Then all you have to do is let the ball get in the way and watch it fly toward your target.

SWING SECTIONS
Backswing: Moving from your address position to the top
Change of Direction: Transitioning from backswing to downswing
Downswing: Continuing your change of direction and swinging down and through impact
End Swing: Moving from impact into a balanced finish position

"THE KEY IS THAT YOU *SWING THE CLUB*. YOU DON'T *HIT A BALL*."

MIKE PERPICH
RiverPines Golf Club, Johns Creek, Ga.
Golf Magazine Top 100 Teacher (2001–present)
● 2011 PGA Growth of the Game Award
(Georgia Section)
● 2004 North Georgia Teacher of the Year
● 1994 PGA Teacher of the Year
(Georgia Section)
● Teaching since 1980
www.mikeperpich.com

PART 1: YOUR BASIC BACKSWING

Think "turn" instead of "lift" and you'll be on the right track.

If you followed the advice in the previous chapter, then it's safe to say that your setup, posture, aim and alignment are solid—if not impeccable. Now the really fun part: starting your swing.

As you were practicing your setup you probably noticed that the club sits on an angle once you sole it on the ground. That angle (the lie of the club) sets the tilt of the circle on which you motion the club per the definition on page 42. **Your job is to swing on this tilted circle from start to finish**, and to do it you need rotation. Your turn—both away from and through the ball—is the heartbeat of your swing.

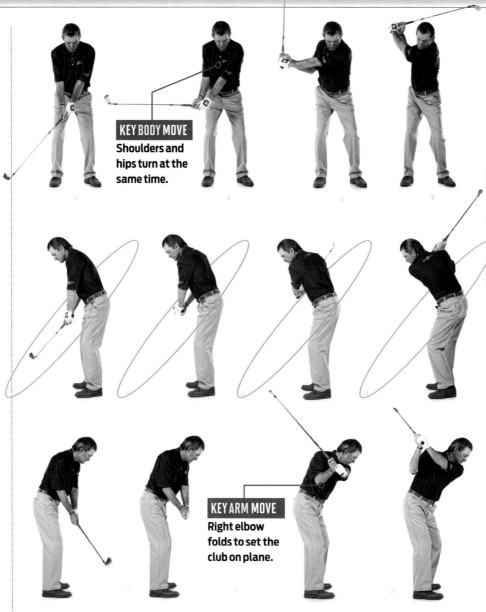

KEY BODY MOVE
Shoulders and hips turn at the same time.

KEY ARM MOVE
Right elbow folds to set the club on plane.

A TURN AND A FOLD
Your move away from the ball sets you up for a smooth transition when you change directions at the top. It includes a unified turn of your shoulders and hips (to create your swing's circle) and a right-elbow fold to set the clubshaft on plane.

At address, focus on your belt buckle and shirt buttons to create a unified turn.

NOTES ON TURNING

Most players think the backswing ends when the arms and club reach a certain point at the top. This leads to overswinging and the gamut of poor shots. Your backswing is complete when your belt buckle and buttons finish turning, and you'll find that they can turn only as far as your flexibility allows.

BACKSWING BODY MOVES

Getting the club to the top is as easy as turning your belt buckle and the buttons on your shirt.

BUTTONS AND BUCKLE

Once you're ready to swing, focus on two points: 1) your belt buckle and 2) the buttons on your shirt. **Begin your motion by turning the buckle and the buttons to the right at the same time and at the same speed without losing the posture you established at address.** Allow your arms and the club to move with your turn. Important: your body is the engine of your swing; your arms and club follow its lead.

Notice that by turning your belt buckle and buttons you're automatically turning your hips and shoulders, respectively. Because each side of your hips and either shoulder can work independently of each other, focusing on the two points pulls everything together and makes it easier to repeat this move successfully under pressure.

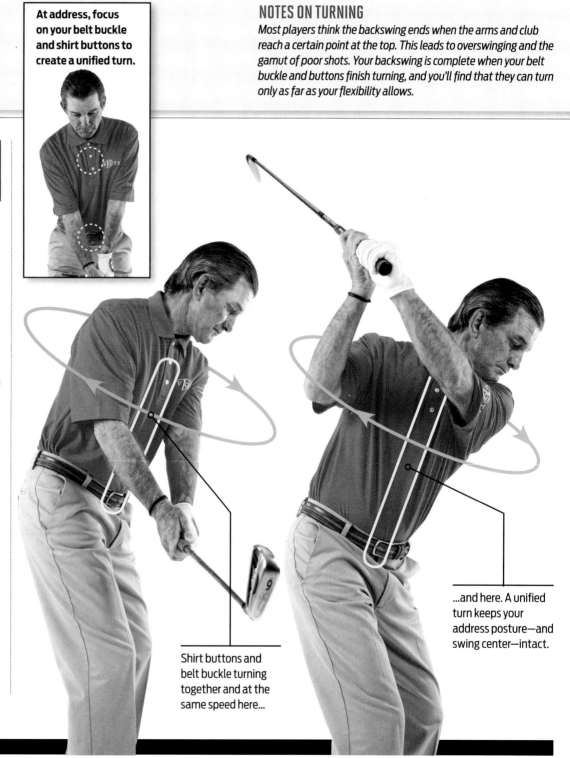

Shirt buttons and belt buckle turning together and at the same speed here...

...and here. A unified turn keeps your address posture—and swing center—intact.

HOW TO GROOVE
A SOLID TURN

This drill not only helps you feel and practice correct backswing rotation, but also increases your flexibility.

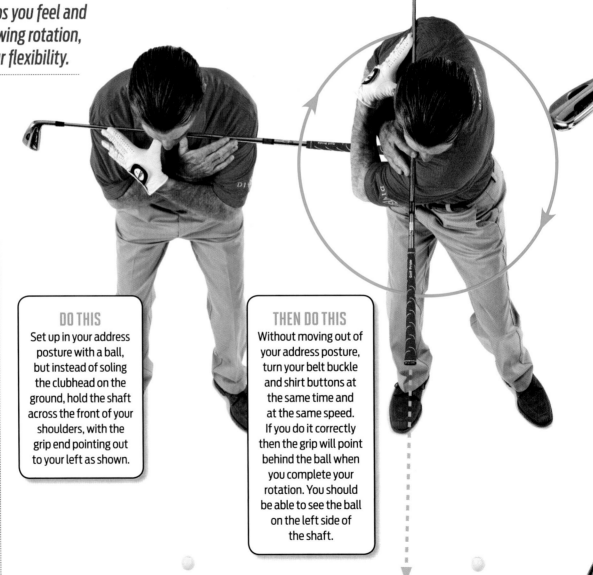

Because your backswing sets the tone for your entire motion, it's critical that you start it correctly by turning your buckle and buttons. I can't overemphasize how important this is, nor how powerful. **If you turn like you're supposed to, then the other parts of your backswing will fall into place as if by magic.** As you practice your turn, mind your posture. The amount you bend forward at address should remain constant. Rotating while staying in your spine angle allows you to coil behind the ball and load your weight onto your right side without your having to think about it. The drill here gives you all the right feels.

DO THIS
Set up in your address posture with a ball, but instead of soling the clubhead on the ground, hold the shaft across the front of your shoulders, with the grip end pointing out to your left as shown.

THEN DO THIS
Without moving out of your address posture, turn your belt buckle and shirt buttons at the same time and at the same speed. If you do it correctly then the grip will point behind the ball when you complete your rotation. You should be able to see the ball on the left side of the shaft.

NOTES ON KNEE FLEX

One of the key factors to turning without disrupting your address posture (i.e., keeping your spine angle intact) is making sure you don't increase or decrease the amount of flex in your right knee. If you do you'll find it impossible to stay in posture. Set the flex at address and then maintain it.

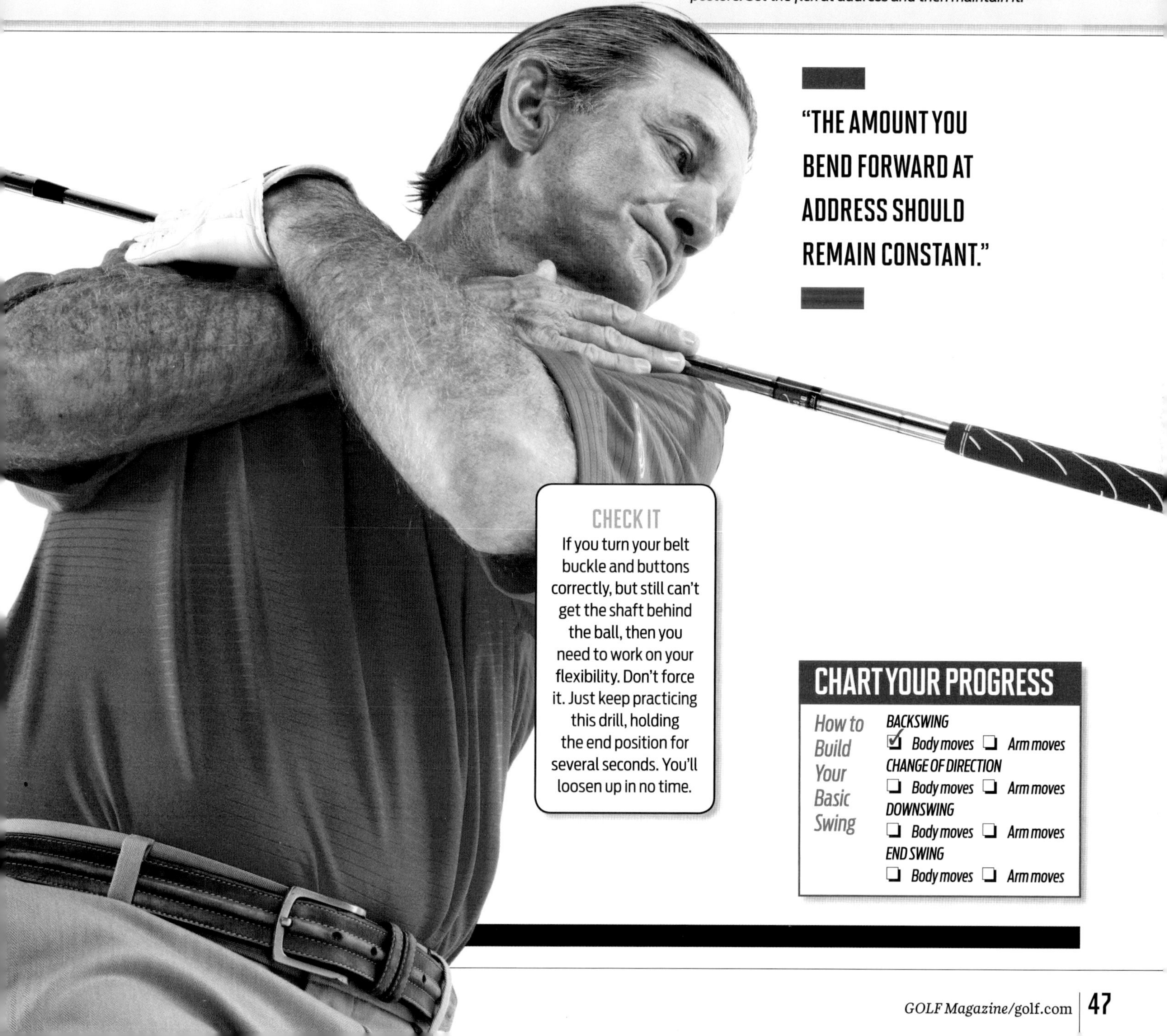

> ## "THE AMOUNT YOU BEND FORWARD AT ADDRESS SHOULD REMAIN CONSTANT."

CHECK IT

If you turn your belt buckle and buttons correctly, but still can't get the shaft behind the ball, then you need to work on your flexibility. Don't force it. Just keep practicing this drill, holding the end position for several seconds. You'll loosen up in no time.

CHART YOUR PROGRESS

How to Build Your Basic Swing

BACKSWING
☑ Body moves ❑ Arm moves
CHANGE OF DIRECTION
❑ Body moves ❑ Arm moves
DOWNSWING
❑ Body moves ❑ Arm moves
END SWING
❑ Body moves ❑ Arm moves

HOW TO
SET THE CLUB ON PLANE

Here's a secret: your arms aren't as important to your backswing as you think.

BACKSWING ARM MOVES

Fold up to stay on the perfect path.

FOCUS ON YOUR RIGHT ELBOW

In building a solid, basic backswing it's important to view your arms as passive. They play a supporting role to the turning action of your belt buckle and shirt buttons, which I discussed on the previous pages. **Your body turns and your arms—along with the club—follow.**

The only move you're required to make with your arms as you turn back is to fold your right elbow. This seemingly simple move creates a whirlwind of action, all of which is very necessary to reach a fundamentally solid position at the top of your backswing.

HOW TO DO IT
Start folding your right elbow as soon as you start turning your buckle and buttons.

Fold your right elbow using a smooth motion, like you're bringing a soda can to your lips (not like you're starting a lawn mower).

Make sure the folding action is constant—do it in perfect time with the turning action of your belt buckle and buttons.

Feel how a smooth folding action causes your left wrist to hinge naturally, giving you an extra lever for power in your swing.

If you turn as you fold, your forearms will rotate smoothly to the right and set the clubshaft and clubface on plane.

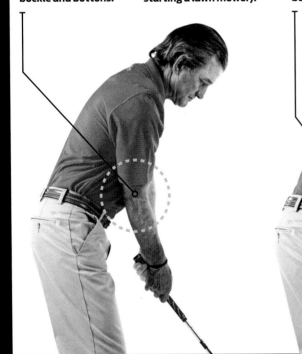

NOTES ON ELBOW FOLD

Folding your right elbow correctly 1) allows your arms to rise up, 2) hinges your left wrist, 3) rotates your forearms clockwise, 4) sets the clubshaft and clubface on plane, 5) supports the weight of the club and your left arm at the top of your backswing and 6) keeps your body and arms connected.

HOW TO GROOVE YOUR ELBOW FOLD

Try this drill to feel how your right arm should bend during your backswing.

1 SET IT

Push a tee into the hole in the cap of the grip, then get into your normal address position.

2 SWING

Turn and fold as shown in the photos on the opposite page.

3 CHECK IT

Stop your swing when your hands reach chest height in your backswing, then take note of the positions at right.

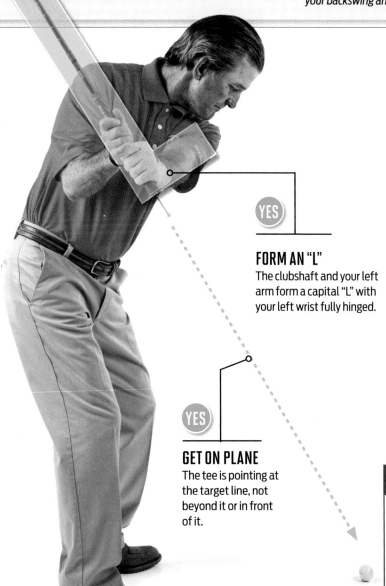

YES

FORM AN "L"

The clubshaft and your left arm form a capital "L" with your left wrist fully hinged.

YES

GET ON PLANE

The tee is pointing at the target line, not beyond it or in front of it.

CAUTION!

As you perform this drill it's important to understand that your clubhead and the grip simply switch positions (one goes up as the other goes down) while staying on the plane established by the lie of the club at address. If you can get this to happen you know you're folding and turning in unison.

CHART YOUR PROGRESS

How to Build Your Basic Swing	BACKSWING	
	☑ Body moves	☑ Arm moves
	CHANGE OF DIRECTION	
	☐ Body moves	☐ Arm moves
	DOWNSWING	
	☐ Body moves	☐ Arm moves
	END SWING	
	☐ Body moves	☐ Arm moves

PART 2:
CHANGING DIRECTION

The smoothest part of your motion can only be smooth if your backswing is sound.

The change of direction portion of your swing is exactly that—a smooth transition between swinging the club back and bringing it down. Unlike your backswing (where everything works together), your change of direction happens in stages. It's more like a sequence of events, the success of which is dependent on the quality of your backswing. **If you don't nail the backswing moves outlined on the previous pages you have almost zero chance of executing a solid change of direction.** Basically, your change of direction involves undoing many of the moves you made in your backswing. Specifically, you'll need to unwind your belt buckle and let the fold out of your right elbow.

KEY BODY MOVE
Hips (belt buckle) separate from shoulders (shirt buttons).

KEY ARM MOVE
Arms fall as right elbow unfolds.

YOUR BASIC CHANGE OF DIRECTION
The change of direction section of your swing is a smooth, unhurried process that should make you feel like the club is falling to the ground as you maintain your forward bend toward the ball.

CHANGE OF DIRECTION BODY MOVES

How to smoothly transition from backswing to downswing and set up a powerful delivery.

TURN YOUR BUCKLE, BUT NOT YOUR BUTTONS

The key to creating a smooth change of direction is separating your hips (your buckle) from your shoulders (your shirt buttons). You do this by unwinding your hips while keeping your shoulders in place. Here's what I mean:

NOTE: You don't need to "fire" your hips at this point in your swing—just unwind them. Remember, all you're doing is changing directions.

END OF BACKSWING
You're balanced and solid because you turned your shirt buttons and belt buckle together.

TRANSITION
Separate your hips from your shoulders by turning your belt buckle to the left without turning your buttons.

HOW TO FEEL IT

If you unwind your hips correctly it should feel like your back is facing the target (like it does at the end of your backswing) even after you start turning your belt buckle. You should also feel weight begin to move from your right side to your left foot, and you start using some of the load and energy you stored up on your backswing.

END OF BACKSWING
Back facing the target here.

TRANSITION
Back still facing the target here.

CHART YOUR PROGRESS

How to Build Your Basic Swing

BACKSWING
☑ Body moves ☑ Arm moves
CHANGE OF DIRECTION
☑ Body moves ☐ Arm moves
DOWNSWING
☐ Body moves ☐ Arm moves
END SWING
☐ Body moves ☐ Arm moves

TRANSITION SECRET:
LET YOUR ARMS FALL

Passive arms allow you to retain the energy in your swing.

T he second of the two primary components of a successful transition is allowing your arms to fall toward the ground while maintaining the "L" formed by your left arm and the clubshaft. **The "L" is key; coincidentally it represents the power lag all great players exploit to hit the ball crisply and with power.** The "L" is stored energy, and the longer you hold it in your downswing (i.e., maintaining it as you change directions), the more power you'll transfer to the ball at impact. Caution! In order for this move to work properly you must stay in your address posture, just like you did during your backswing.

CHANGE OF DIRECTION ARM MOVES

Keeping the club on plane as you start down is simply a matter of giving in to gravity.

DROP AND UNFOLD
As you begin to unwind your belt buckle (hips), it will feel as if your left arm is falling toward the ground—a passive "act" that adds to the smoothness of your transition. If you do it correctly the "L" will remain intact. Some players confuse the drop move by keeping both arms passive. That'll just stick the club behind you and too far under the correct plane. **The trick is to drop your left arm (maintaining the "L") while letting out the fold in your right elbow.** Let it out smoothly and in time with the dropping action of your left arm. If you rush it you'll lose the "L."

Left arm dropping down.

Belt buckle unwinding.

HOW TO GIVE IN TO GRAVITY

STEP 1
Make your regular backswing and stop at the top.

STEP 2
Without moving anything else, slide your right hand to the bottom of the grip.

STEP 3
Unwind your belt buckle while allowing your arms to fall in front of you. Notice how the split grip makes it easy to feel and maintain the "L" in your swing (the connection between your left arm and the clubshaft), even as you straighten your right arm. Do it in slow motion, and don't forget to turn your belt buckle.

Right elbow smoothly unfolding.

"L" between shaft and left arm intact.

Both arms dropping yet staying in front of the body.

"L" still intact—energy remains stored.

Right elbow continues unfolding.

CHART YOUR PROGRESS

How to Build Your Basic Swing

BACKSWING		
☑ Body moves	☑ Arm moves	
CHANGE OF DIRECTION		
☑ Body moves	☑ Arm moves	
DOWNSWING		
❑ Body moves	❑ Arm moves	
END SWING		
❑ Body moves	❑ Arm moves	

PART 3:
YOUR BASIC DOWNSWING

Follow three key basics to strike the ball squarely and with speed.

Since your downswing picks up right in the middle of your change of direction, its primary principles—what you need to follow as you move into impact—include much of what you learned in the previous section: 1) hips continue to unwind, 2) the "L" between your left arm and clubshaft continues to fall and 3) everything happens without disrupting your original spine angle.

Notice that I didn't say much about your hands, arms or the club. These elements continue to remain passive, and the dynamics of a solid impact position happen as if by magic if you simply follow the key downswing basics.

KEY BODY MOVE
Hips continue unwinding as you stay in your posture.

KEY ARM MOVE
Right elbow continues to unfold as the "L" continues to drop.

A MATTER OF UNWINDING
Your backswing is all about storing energy. You make a downswing to expend it, but the goal remains the same: keep unwinding your body.

DOWNSWING BODY MOVES

You may be tempted to control what the club is doing as you swing down. Fight the urge. If you continue to unwind correctly the club will follow suit.

TURN, DON'T SPIN

The biggest part of your downswing is your turn. Your primary goal in this section of your swing is to continue unwinding your hips through impact and ultimately into your finish. The reason why most players can't get to a solid impact position is because they don't turn correctly, or they *spin* instead of *unwind*. These terms sound an awful lot alike, but they're two completely different things. **Spinning invokes the image of a top, rotating in one place. Unwinding means turning your belt buckle in such a way that your weight naturally moves from your right leg to your left as you do it.**

Here's a great way to acquire the proper feel for how your hips should unwind and turn on the downswing.

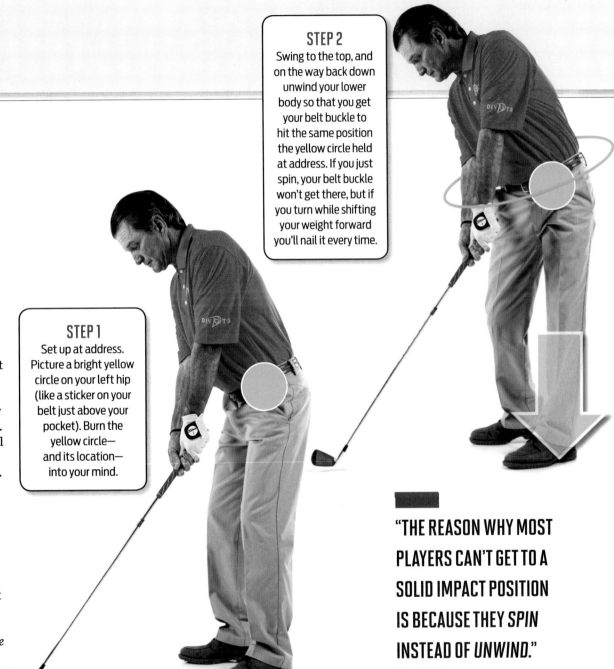

STEP 1
Set up at address. Picture a bright yellow circle on your left hip (like a sticker on your belt just above your pocket). Burn the yellow circle— and its location— into your mind.

STEP 2
Swing to the top, and on the way back down unwind your lower body so that you get your belt buckle to hit the same position the yellow circle held at address. If you just spin, your belt buckle won't get there, but if you turn while shifting your weight forward you'll nail it every time.

"THE REASON WHY MOST PLAYERS CAN'T GET TO A SOLID IMPACT POSITION IS BECAUSE THEY *SPIN* INSTEAD OF *UNWIND*."

HOW TO CHECK
YOUR DOWNSWING TURN

Replace your left hip with your right hip.

Turning your hips correctly using the images and feels on this and the previous page gets you into a solid impact position without your having to think about it. You don't "do" an impact—it's something that happens, and the better you are at turning your hips correctly the better your impact will be.

All of the positions good players achieve when they make contact with the ball happen because of proper hip motion and not because of anything they do with their hands or arms. It's that simple. The moment you start forcing the club into position as you swing through the ball is the moment you start hitting unpredictable shots. Your turn takes care of everything.

CHECK THIS

Make a few practice swings, paying extra attention to your left and right hips. (We've mostly treated your hips as a single unit thus far by focusing on your belt buckle, but for the purposes of this drill we'll split them apart.) Your goal on each of these swings is to get your right hip into the spot your left hip holds at the top of your backswing and do it by the time you reach your finish (*photos, below*). Rotating your hips in this manner (continue using your belt buckle as a guide) will create a solid impact position almost automatically.

PROPER HIP ROTATION...

● Gets your weight moving forward so it's mostly on your front foot at impact.
● **Squares the clubface at impact.**
● Gets the shaft leaning toward the target at impact with your hands ahead of the clubhead.
● **Helps you contact the ball in the center of the sweet spot.**
● Makes the back of your left hand flat like it should be at impact.
● **Creates a divot in front of the ball (with your irons) or an upward strike (with your driver).**

Left hip in the box here.

Right hip in the box here.

HIP REPLACEMENT
Unwind your body so that your right hip gets to the position your left hip holds at the top of your backswing. This ensures a full and constant turn.

A NOTE ON KNEE ACTION

As you swing down from the top and through impact, let the flex out of your left knee, timing it so that your left leg goes perfectly straight the moment the ball leaves the clubface. "Posting" like this gives your hips the room they need to properly unwind all the way to the finish.

HOW TO PRACTICE A PROPER TURN

My go get it drill is the ultimate practice routine to capture the true, realistic motion of how your body works on your downswing and through impact into the finish.

NO

A COMMON ERROR

If you try to put your right hand back on the club by only swinging your right arm, you'll never get there. You can only go get it if you unwind your hips. They're the engines that take you where you need to go on your downswing.

1 SET UP

Get into your address position with any one of your mid-irons. You won't need to hit a ball with this drill.

2 POINT

Without moving anything else, extend your left arm and club down the target line. You want your shaft and forearm as close to horizontal as possible with the toe of the club pointing up.

3 GO GET IT!

While keeping your left arm and club in place, reach for the grip and reset your right hand on the handle. Notice how you instinctively shift your weight and turn your lower body to get your right hand on the club again.

HOW TO MAINTAIN YOUR POSTURE

Lose your spine angle and your forward tilt as you swing down and you'll lose a lot of balls.

One—if not the biggest—factor that helps you achieve a solid impact position is staying in the posture you establish at address. The degree to which you bend over toward the ball and tilt your spine away from the target at address sets the center point of your swing. Remember our definition? Your swing is a circular movement around a fixed central point, and if you move out of your posture you'll move your center, which will then force you to compensate for the change. In golf, compensations lead to errors, inconsistency and loss of power and accuracy.

The key to maintaining your posture is simply adhering to the basics. Losing your spine angle or forward tilt is an indication that one of these basics isn't being followed. If this is you, go back and use the checkpoints in this chapter, focusing on your body and not your hands or club.

The posture you establish at setup...

...should still be intact when you strike the ball.

SPINE ANGLE
The distance between the center of your chest and the ball never changes.

PRACTICE ON A SLANT
Tilt your hitting area to help maintain
your posture when you swing.

Full swing video lessons at **golf.com/instruction**
and on the tablet editions of Golf Magazine

1 ADDRESS
Find a sloping section
of ground off to the
side of the range so that
you can make practice
swings with the ball above
your feet.

2 BACKSWING
The hill emphasizes
the need to maintain
your forward bend. Notice
how you stay in your tilt
by matching the angle
your torso made with the
ground at address with the
left side of your body at
the top.

> "LOSING YOUR SPINE ANGLE IS AN INDICATION THAT ONE OF THESE BASICS ISN'T BEING FOLLOWED."

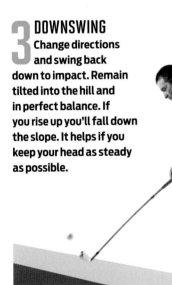

3 DOWNSWING
Change directions
and swing back
down to impact. Remain
tilted into the hill and
in perfect balance. If
you rise up you'll fall down
the slope. It helps if you
keep your head as steady
as possible.

4 FINISH
End your swing with
your weight on your
left leg and you knees
and thighs touching.
If you maintain your
tilt correctly, your body
will be angled the same
amount it was at address,
but with your right side
facing the ground instead
of your chest.

CHART YOUR PROGRESS

How to Build Your Basic Swing		
BACKSWING		
☑ Body moves	☑ Arm moves	
CHANGE OF DIRECTION		
☑ Body moves	☑ Arm moves	
DOWNSWING		
☑ Body moves	☐ Arm moves	
END SWING		
☐ Body moves	☐ Arm moves	

HOW TO
SWING INTO IMPACT

Connect your arms to your body and then let your body do all the work.

I like to think of the arms as simply attachments to all that your body is doing. They're like a couple pieces of rope loosely connected to your shoulders. They play an important role in that they connect the club to your body, but are nonetheless followers of action, not leaders.

This is a concept most players have a hard time getting their heads around because they're so used to executing motions with their hands and arms—throwing a football, shooting a basketball, etc. But their role really is to respond to your turn. It's not a simplified concept. It's a correct one. **Golfers who worry about where the shaft is or where the clubface is pointing are doomed to a lifetime of bad swings and scores.**

Important: connect your arms to your body so that they can more easily follow your turn. Feel like your upper left arm is snug and across your chest as you take the club up and then back down.

DOWNSWING ARM MOVES

Connect your arms to your turn instead of swinging them.

CONNECT HERE
Maintain contact between your upper left arm and the left side of your chest from address all the way through impact.

FOLLOW HERE
The only active move your right arm makes in your downswing is to straighten and get the fold out of your elbow.

*Impact video lessons at **golf.com/contact**
and on the tablet editions of* Golf Magazine

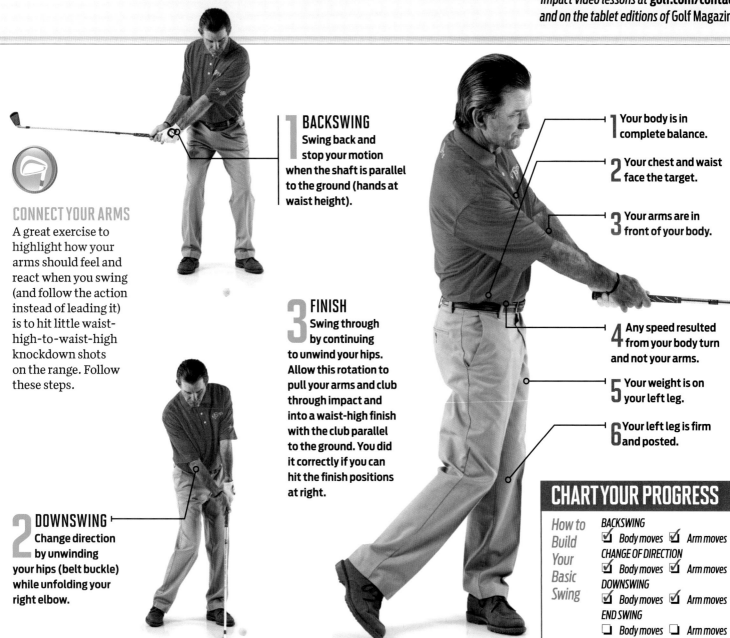

CONNECT YOUR ARMS

A great exercise to highlight how your arms should feel and react when you swing (and follow the action instead of leading it) is to hit little waist-high-to-waist-high knockdown shots on the range. Follow these steps.

1 BACKSWING
Swing back and stop your motion when the shaft is parallel to the ground (hands at waist height).

2 DOWNSWING
Change direction by unwinding your hips (belt buckle) while unfolding your right elbow.

3 FINISH
Swing through by continuing to unwind your hips. Allow this rotation to pull your arms and club through impact and into a waist-high finish with the club parallel to the ground. You did it correctly if you can hit the finish positions at right.

1 Your body is in complete balance.

2 Your chest and waist face the target.

3 Your arms are in front of your body.

4 Any speed resulted from your body turn and not your arms.

5 Your weight is on your left leg.

6 Your left leg is firm and posted.

CHART YOUR PROGRESS

How to Build Your Basic Swing		
BACKSWING		
☑ Body moves	☑ Arm moves	
CHANGE OF DIRECTION		
☑ Body moves	☑ Arm moves	
DOWNSWING		
☑ Body moves	☑ Arm moves	
END SWING		
❏ Body moves	❏ Arm moves	

PART 4:
FINISHING YOUR SWING

Cutting your rotation short means ruining all the good things that came before it.

At this point, the heavy lifting in your swing is over. Moving from impact into your finish position mostly concerns continuing your rotation—**if there's a point I should be hammering in this chapter it's that you never stop rotating.** Don't stop turning until your body tells you to stop turning. Even though the ball is well on its way, you still need rotation to achieve a full, balanced finish and to keep the club swinging on plane on the target side of your swing.

If you do this you'll automatically get all of your weight on your left leg with your knees and thighs touching and your right foot balancing on its toe. These are the traits of a solid, balanced finish.

KEY BODY MOVE
Hips unwind, spine angle maintained.

END SWING
Continuing your rotation after impact and into your finish position is what keeps the club swinging on the proper plane and your body in complete balance.

KEY ARM MOVE
Left elbow folds, hinging the club on plane.

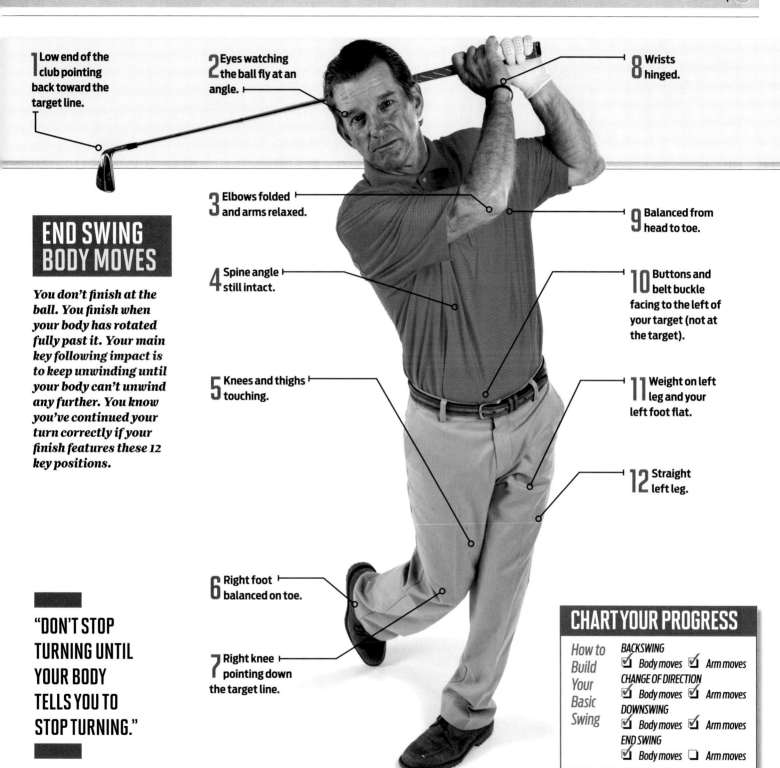

1 Low end of the club pointing back toward the target line.

2 Eyes watching the ball fly at an angle.

8 Wrists hinged.

3 Elbows folded and arms relaxed.

9 Balanced from head to toe.

4 Spine angle still intact.

10 Buttons and belt buckle facing to the left of your target (not at the target).

5 Knees and thighs touching.

11 Weight on left leg and your left foot flat.

12 Straight left leg.

6 Right foot balanced on toe.

7 Right knee pointing down the target line.

END SWING BODY MOVES

You don't finish at the ball. You finish when your body has rotated fully past it. Your main key following impact is to keep unwinding until your body can't unwind any further. You know you've continued your turn correctly if your finish features these 12 key positions.

"DON'T STOP TURNING UNTIL YOUR BODY TELLS YOU TO STOP TURNING."

CHART YOUR PROGRESS

How to Build Your Basic Swing		
BACKSWING		
☑ Body moves	☑ Arm moves	
CHANGE OF DIRECTION		
☑ Body moves	☑ Arm moves	
DOWNSWING		
☑ Body moves	☑ Arm moves	
END SWING		
☑ Body moves	☐ Arm moves	

MUST-HAVE MOVES TO
FINISH ON PLANE

Think of your through-swing as a mirror image of your backswing to keep it moving on the correct path.

One of the key arm moves in your backswing is folding your right elbow (*page 48*), a move that hinges your wrists and sets the club on the correct plane. Since you never want to fall off plane, even after the ball already is on its way, you need to fold your left elbow as you unwind to the finish. **Folding your left elbow in your through-swing rehinges your wrists and allows the clubhead to move up the correct exit plane (i.e., keeps your swing on its circle).** Eventually your right elbow will fold to match your left as your swing loses momentum and your arms fall into a resting position. This doesn't sound very athletic, but it's a good feeling to have. Watch any Tour pro and you'll see him or her swing with maximum energy at impact to almost zero just milliseconds later in his or her finish.

END SWING ARM MOVES

Your left elbow must fold, just like your right did on your backswing.

PRACTICE CROSS-HANDED
One of the best drills to help you groove a fluid through-swing is to make practice swings using a cross-handed (left-hand-low) grip. **Holding the club this way makes it much easier to fold your left elbow as you move into the target side of your swing.** Take your cross-handed grip and simply make smooth practice swings back and through. Notice how your left elbow folds almost automatically and how your wrists respond by hinging freely. As you get the hang of it, tee up some balls and hit practice shots. You might find yourself hitting a nice draw after a while.

DRILL BONUS

Swinging cross-handed also accentuates the feeling of your arms falling as you change direction from backswing to downswing. You'll also notice how much easier it is to unwind your hips from the top all the way to your finish. That's because of the increased falling action—you turn easier when you don't try to "hit" the ball.

*Swing drills and video tips at **golf.com/instruction** and on the tablet editions of Golf Magazine*

NO ## DON'T DO THIS

The dreaded "chicken wing"! I've gone back to my regular grip, but notice how I've failed to fold my left elbow. Instead, it's bent and pointing down the target line. Also notice how my hips have stopped rotating, which will make it impossible for me to end this swing on plane and in balance. The bad thing about chicken-winging is that you can't do it without having the clubface open at impact. (Hello, slice.) **Stopping your rotation is one way to produce a chicken wing. You can also make this error by overusing your arms and making them leaders instead of followers.** Most recreational players allow this to happen by failing to correctly drop their arms from the top and maintain the "L" during their change of direction. When the body and arms reverse roles like this, you'll chicken-wing it every time.

CHART YOUR PROGRESS

How to Build Your Basic Swing		
BACKSWING		
☑ Body moves	☑ Arm moves	
CHANGE OF DIRECTION		
☑ Body moves	☑ Arm moves	
DOWNSWING		
☑ Body moves	☑ Arm moves	
END SWING		
☑ Body moves	☑ Arm moves	

PART 5:
PUTTING IT ALL TOGETHER

Smoothly blending body and arm motions creates a unified, flowing swing that places the clubshaft, clubface and clubhead in perfect position from start to finish.

began our discussion about the swing by giving you a very simple definition (*page 42*) to help you understand its core principles. I — showed you how to put your swing in motion by breaking it down into separate sections, and within each part of this chapter I have distilled it even further by focusing only on key body and arm movements. It's now time for the finishing touches: how to combine the sections and movements into a smooth, flowing motion that's both consistent and repeatable. Only when you unify all the sections of your swing will you start to make your swing your own.

That's not to say that our approach thus far has been for naught. It's critical that you work on the areas covered in these pages step-by-step. **But there comes a time when you should start using these positions as checkpoints instead of swing keys.** Continue to use them to help guide you into the right angles and motions when you practice (and to check that your body, arms and club are where they need to be at every moment in your swing), but with an eye toward blending everything together to create a unified motion that's fit to put into play.

To help you better understand how everything comes together, forget the technical aspects for a moment and picture with your mind's eye the image of a child playing on a swing set on a playground. Picture the chair generating power as it swings back, smoothly changes directions and then speeds forward. Keeping this image in mind is a good way to get out of "position" golf and create a smooth, flowing, unified motion.

PLAY THE MATCH GAME

Once you're capable of executing the key body and arm moves, you'll start to realize that your swing is basically a series of alternating parallel shaft positions (*photos, below*). Important: even though we're talking about shaft positions in this checkpoint, never try to force the clubshaft into place. It gets to where it needs to go when you execute fundamentally solid body and arm moves. Nonetheless, checking your motion (preferably in a mirror) and making sure you're hitting these shaft positions is a productive way to unify your motion.

ADDRESS
Shaft parallel to swing plane.

TAKEAWAY
Shaft parallel to ground.

BACKSWING
Shaft parallel to swing plane.

TOP POSITION
Shaft parallel to ground.

CHANGE OF DIRECTION
Shaft parallel to swing plane.

DOWNSWING
Shaft parallel to ground.

IMPACT
Shaft parallel to swing plane.

RELEASE
Shaft parallel to ground.

THROUGH-SWING
Shaft parallel to swing plane.

FINISH
Shaft parallel to ground (then wrapped around).

THE EASY WAY TO
MAKE YOUR SWING WORK

Your backswing starts your motion, so errors here are likely to damage every part of your swing that follows.

A successful swing is one that motions the club on plane, because **staying on plane creates the least amount of resistance when you swing.** The moment your club, hands and arms move out of the correct positions is the moment when you have to fight to get things where they need to be at impact. Those are the days when your swing feels sluggish and difficult to repeat and you feel out of balance from start to finish.

The more you learn about your swing, the more you'll realize that starting it correctly by matching up body and arm moves as you go from address to the top is what allows you to swing the club on plane from start to finish. Let's just say it's easier to hit the right checkpoints on your downswing, at impact and beyond if you hit the right ones in your backswing. Correcting backswing errors when they pop up in your motion is vital for long-term success.

RECHECK YOUR TURN AND FOLD

Take the club back and hold. Use a mirror to see if you're matching the positions in the photo at right. These backswing positions are critical for overall success.

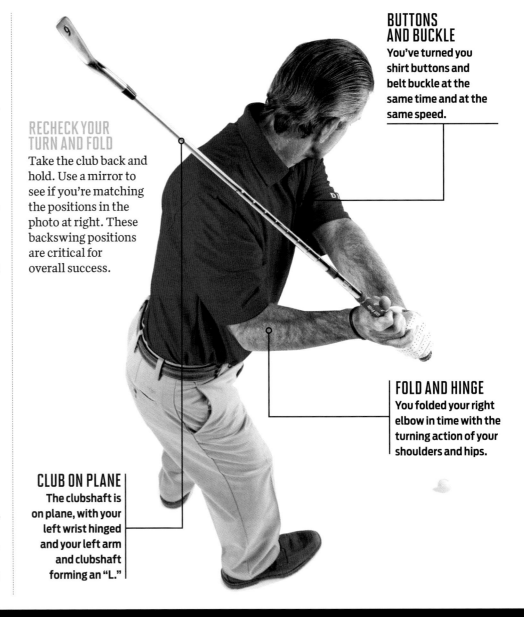

BUTTONS AND BUCKLE
You've turned you shirt buttons and belt buckle at the same time and at the same speed.

FOLD AND HINGE
You folded your right elbow in time with the turning action of your shoulders and hips.

CLUB ON PLANE
The clubshaft is on plane, with your left wrist hinged and your left arm and clubshaft forming an "L."

DON'T DO THIS

Avoid these two common backswing errors. Committing these gets you off track at the very start.

ROLLING FOREARMS

Starting your swing by rolling your hands instead of turning your shoulders and hips sets the club under plane. It will also force you to lose your spine tilt by standing or straightening up.

TURNING HANDS

Pulling your arms back and turning your hands under (counterclockwise) cause your left shoulder to dip instead of turn. Now you've reverse-pivoted with the clubshaft too far above plane.

AVOID THE OVERSWING

The most common backswing error is overswinging, or going past the natural end of your turn. The end of your backswing is a critical area in that it's the point when the change of direction starts. Delaying it disrupts your entire transition and, as you can guess, the rest of your swing.

Your backswing ends when your belt buckle and buttons can no longer turn. You'll know when you reach this point—and if you go past it—if you start losing your spine angle.

One of the goals in your swing is to keep the club on plane from start to finish, and it immediately falls off once you swing past your natural end point.

Rehearse your backswing in slow motion to find out when your turn comes to its end, and burn the sensation into your body and mind. Gradually add speed. You'll eventually come to a point when it's too fast to stop at your spot. **The secret is to find the pace that allows you to match up your motions and actions while staying in your spine angle.**

BIG-TIME ERROR

Swinging past your natural stopping point disrupts your transition and makes it almost impossible to achieve a solid impact position.

REVIEW: PARTS OF THE WHOLE

Understanding how body and arm movements combine to create your overall motion is key to putting it all together and building a consistent and reliable swing.

1 **Always work and check on your body first. Forget about the club.**

2 Your turn is the heart and soul of your swing. When in doubt, remember your buttons and buckle.

3 **A fundamentally sound swing produces power and accuracy, and maintaining your spine angle will help you achieve both of these.**

4 Your arms and hands are attachments. Your arms react to your turn.

5 **Folding you right elbow builds the "L" on the backswing. Unfolding it allows your arms to fall when you change directions.**

6 Folding your left elbow in your through-swing keeps the club on plane on the target side of your swing.

7 **Work on the basics in segments: address, backswing, change of direction, downswing and finish. Take one part at a time.**

8 Work on you, not what you're doing. Regardless of the move you're practicing, go at it using a speed that allows you to monitor your actions. Once you feel like you're getting it, add speed. Then, introduce a golf ball. Work in steps—you can't rush the basics.

THE ULTIMATE
BACKSWING FIX GUIDE

How to check for errors in your backswing and top position and then pinpoint the drills you need to get back on track.

SPOT THE FAULTS

If any of the errors on this page and the next look familiar, then you need to get back to the basic skills in this chapter to fix them for good or you'll never shoot the scores you desire.

PULLING, NOT FOLDING

Cause: Snatching the club back with your hands and arms.
Result: Misses both ways, toe hits, power loss.
Fix: Turn drill (*p. 46*), Sidehill drill (*p. 59*).

DIPPING UNDER

Cause: Pulling teh club back with the arms while dipping the left shoulder.
Result: Blocks to the right, hooks.
Fix: Turn drill (*p. 46*), Right Elbow drill (*p. 49*).

NO ELBOW FOLD

Cause: Arms controlling turn.
Result: Loss of power, short-game problems.
Fix: Right Elbow drill (*p. 49*).

TOO VERTICAL

Cause: You stopped your turn and lifted your arms.
Result: Over-the-top (cut) swing, pull-hooks, slices.
Fix: Buttons and Buckle lesson (*p. 45*), Turn drill (*p. 46*).

TOO FLAT

Cause: Stopping your shoulder turn and standing up.
Result: Over-swinging, poor contact.
Fix: Turn drill (*p. 46*), Sidehill drill (*p. 59*)

BALL-FLIGHT GUIDE

1. **Straight:** Path on line, face square
2. **Hook:** Path along line, face closed
3. **Slice:** Path along line, face open
4. **Pull:** Path out-in, face square to path
5. **Pull-hook:** Path out-in, face closed to path
6. **Pull-slice:** Path out-in, face open to path
7. **Push:** Path in-out, face square to path
8. **Push-hook:** Path in-out, face closed to path
9. **Push-slice:** Path in-out, face open to path

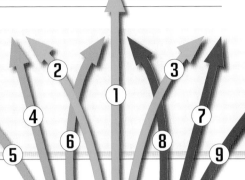

ALL ARMS, NO TURN

Cause: You forgot to turn your buttons and buckle.
Result: Off-plane swing, loss of power, thin and fat shots.
Fix: Buttons and Buckle lesson (p. 45).

OUTSIDE PUSH

Cause: Trying to create extra width by pushing the arms out.
Result: Poor balance and swing path, overswinging.
Fix: Turn drill (p. 46), Right Elbow drill (p. 49).

FAKE TURN

Cause: Arms pull back so hard that you feel like you're turning.
Result: Loss of power and spine angle, poor swing path.
Fix: Right Elbow drill (p. 49).

ACROSS THE LINE

Cause: Bad right elbow fold.
Result: Over-swinging, poor change of direction.
Fix: Right Elbow drill (p. 49).

LAID OFF

Cause: Loss of spine tilt.
Result: Poor change of direction, fat and thin contact.
Fix: Sidehill drill (p. 59).

THE ULTIMATE
DOWNSWING FIX GUIDE

Look for these common backswing and through-swing errors, then consult the drills to eliminate them from your motion.

KEEP IT SIMPLE

Most of the errors pictured here result from improper use of your hands and arms. Get back to your body basics and you'll start to see better arm and hand (as well as shaft and clubhead positions) throughout your motion.

SPINOUT
Cause: You turned your buttons instead of your buckle.
Result: Pulls, pull-slices, slices.
Fix: Separation drill (p. 51).

CASTING
Cause: You lost the "L."
Result: Loss of power, poor swing path.
Fix: Split Grip drill (p. 53); Separation drill (p. 51).

FAKE LAG
Cause: You dropped your arms, but you didn't unfold your right elbow.
Result: Pushes, loss of power.
Fix: Split Grip drill (p. 53).

CROWDING
Cause: Standing up through impact.
Result: Loss of power, poor contact, loss of balance.
Fix: Go Get It drill (p. 57), Knockdown drill (p. 61).

HANGING BACK
Cause: You stopped unwinding.
Result: Thin shots, low shots, loss of power.
Fix: Unwinding drill (p. 56), Knockdown Drill (p. 61).

Video lessons to fix every flaw at **golf.com/instruction**
and on the tablet editions of Golf Magazine

INSIDE DELIVERY

Cause: You failed to unfold your right elbow.
Result: Pushes, fat shots, snap hooks.
Fix: Sidehill drill (*p. 59*), Arms Falling drill (*p. 53*).

THROWAWAY

Cause: Poor change of direction.
Result: Complete power loss.
Fix: Arms Falling drill (*p. 53*), Split Grip drill (*p. 53*).

SLIDING

Cause: Leaning instead of unwinding.
Result: Loss of power, mushy contact.
Fix: Don't Spin drill (*p. 55*), Unwinding drill (*p. 56*).

EARLY RELEASE

Cause: Poor change of direction.
Result: Total power loss.
Fix: Split Grip drill (*p. 53*); Arms Falling drill (*p. 53*).

POOR TURN

Cause: Stopping your body at the ball (i.e., trying to "hit" it).
Result: Low shots, slices, power loss.
Fix: Go Get It drill (*p. 57*), Cross Handed drill (*p. 64*).

FAKE FINISH

Cause: Right hip failed to replace left hip.
Result: Inconsistency, slices, hooks, power loss.
Fix: Split Grip drill (*p. 53*), Go Get It drill (*p. 57*).

ADD POWER TO YOUR DRIVER AND WOODS

How to tweak your basic setup and swing to take advantage of the longer clubs in your bag and become the biggest hitter in your foursome

KEY CHANGES FOR YOUR
DRIVER, WOODS & HYBRIDS

INSIDE
Three ways to learn
the basics you need:

LESSONS
Tips and instruction
to help you master
fundamental moves
and positions

CHECKPOINTS
Tests to see if you're
keeping up or falling
behind in your quest to
build a better game

DRILLS
Practice tips and
step-by-step exercises
to make new moves
second nature

Your driver, fairway woods and hybrids are longer and faster than the rest of your clubs. You need a few extra basics to max out their potential.

Drivers, fairway woods and hybrids are physically different from irons in that they have longer shafts, flatter lie angles and larger heads with centers of gravity well away from the clubface. Due to these differences they require significant modifications in your basic setup and swing technique in order to perform effectively.

Irons are designed to hit the ball with a descending blow and with a forward leaning shaft on a fairly upright plane. (You have all that you need to make these things happen thanks to the lessons you learned with fellow *Golf Magazine* Top 100 Teachers Lou Guzzi and Mike Perpich in chapters 1 and 2, respectively.) In contrast, a driver needs to move on a flatter plane and strike the ball

on the upswing. Fairway woods and hybrids fall somewhere in between but definitely require a swing that differs slightly from the one you use to hit your irons. Yes, in golf you need two swings: one for irons and wedges and another for woods and driver.

To adjust your swing to effectively hit a driver, you'll need to change your setup so that your right shoulder is noticeably lower than your left. You'll have to get into the habit of playing the ball more forward in your stance and making a conscious effort to tilt your upper body away from the target (spine leaning right). These changes—and more— are necessary to promote an ascending strike on the ball when you're hitting driver. Fairway woods and hybrids will require slightly less significant adjustments, but important ones nonetheless.

On the following pages I'll show you how to make the necessary setup and swing and also provide some basic drills to help you groove them without too much effort. As you progress through the chapter, make sure you have each alteration correct before moving on to the drills. If you pay attention and follow the instruction in proper order, I guarantee improved performance.

> "IN GOLF YOU
> NEED TWO SWINGS:
> ONE FOR IRONS
> AND WEDGES
> AND ANOTHER
> FOR WOODS
> AND DRIVER."

YOUR POWER TRAINER

GOLF MAGAZINE TOP 100 TEACHERS IN AMERICA

BRIAN MANZELLA
Brian Manzella Golf Academy,
English Turn Golf & C.C., New Orleans, La.
Golf Magazine Top 100 Teacher (2011–present)
● 2003 PGA Teacher of the Year
(Kentucky Section)
● Director, Golf Teaching Excellence seminars
● Teaching since 1989
www.brianmanzella.com

PART 1:
MAXIMIZING YOUR DRIVER

Copy the positions you see here and you'll drive the ball high, far and straight.

The secret to hitting a driver long and straight is to **contact the ball slightly on the upswing and produce a shot that launches high and with a relatively low amount of spin.** Although many aspects of the general swing technique you learned in Chapter 2 apply to your driver motion, it's critical that you understand the key difference, which is that you hit up into the ball with a driver and hit down on the ball with an iron. Your setup plays a big part in creating the proper, ascending strike.

NO
Placing too much weight on your front foot and shifting your shoulders and spine toward the target will make it impossible to hit the ball on the upswing.

1. HEAD POSITION
Should be level and well behind the ball. Your nose should be just inside of your right knee.

2. HAND POSITION
Set your hands in the middle of your body so the shaft of your driver leans slightly away from the target. Check that there's the same amount of leg visible to the side of each arm.

3. BALL POSITION
Must be well forward, off your left heel and slightly forward of your left shoulder.

"YOU HIT UP INTO THE BALL WITH A DRIVER AND HIT DOWN ON THE BALL WITH AN IRON."

7. SHOULDER POSITION

Your right shoulder should sit well below your left shoulder. This is key to creating an upward strike on the ball. Tilt your upper body like this without tilting your hips, which should remain level.

NO

Setting up with open shoulders (pointing left of target) encourages a steep swing—not what you want with a driver.

NO

Spine tilted to the left with right hip higher than left.

4. ARM POSITION

Because you're tilting away from the target (*see No. 7, right*), your left arm should be a bit higher than your right. Again, this is to help promote an ascending swing into the ball.

6. SHAFT POSITION

The shaft of the club should point at your belt line. The driver has to swing on a relatively flat plane and this will get you going in the right direction.

5. FOOT POSITION

Your right foot should be pulled back slightly behind your left foot.

NOTES ON ADDRESS

Setting up behind the ball with square to slightly closed shoulders and hips and your hands in the middle of your body gives you the best chance to swing on a flatter plane and contact the ball slightly on the upswing.

HOW TO NAIL YOUR DRIVER SETUP

Two simple drills to make sure your starting position is sound.

Just as is the case with irons, to hit your driver solidly you'll have to start with the proper setup position. The real keys to remember are making sure you have a forward ball position, that your shoulders and hips are square or slightly closed, and that your spine is tilted away from the target so your right shoulder is lower than your left (*see pages 78-79*). Here are two drills to make sure you've got it right.

DRILL 1: FACE THE CLUBHEAD

Most golfers instinctively set up while facing the ball. With a driver, this instinct often leads to a setup that features open shoulders and hips, a head position that's too far forward and shoulders tilted to the left. These mistakes create a lot of problems that lead to weak shots.

To practice setting up properly, tee up a ball off your left instep and slightly ahead of your left shoulder, and then ignore it. Set up as if the ball is more in the center of your stance, with square shoulders and hips and a head position that's neutral and level (*photo, above left*). Once you're properly set up, simply slide the clubhead over to the ball without changing anything else (*above right*). Now you should have an ideal driver setup position.

DRILL 2: SWING YOUR RIGHT ARM

Another simple way to ensure you get set up properly is to grip the club with your left hand only at address.

1 LET IT HANG
Tee the ball in the correct spot (off your left instep and ahead of your left shoulder) and then set up to it with your right arm behind your right thigh.

2 SWING IT IN
Once you're set, with square shoulders and hips, swing your right hand over so it's approaching the grip. You should feel your right shoulder dip quite a bit lower than your left.

3 FINISH IT OFF
Swing your right hand all the way up onto the handle and then grip the club with both hands. This is the position you want to be in every time, with your hips level and your right shoulder noticeably below your left.

MAKE SURE YOU'RE BEHIND THE BALL

If you're wondering why it's critical to get your head well behind the ball at setup, it's actually pretty simple. The lowest point in the swing with a driver normally occurs between your left ear and left shoulder. If your head moves forward so it's near this area, you'll be forced to swing down very steeply on the ball and hit it with a descending blow. Not what you want. If you don't start your head well behind the ball, and keep it there, you'll have to make a sudden move backward as the clubhead nears impact, which is low percentage at best.

THE BALL
Set it just ahead of your left shoulder.

YOUR HEAD
Set it just inside your right knee.

YOUR BASIC
DRIVER TAKEAWAY

Turn—don't tilt— your shoulders to swing the club on a flatter plane.

When you're working on your driver technique you must remember that one of the basic differences between a driver and an iron swing is the driver needs to move on a flatter plane because it's much longer, and it needs to swing up into the ball, not down, at impact. The takeaway section of your swing sets up the rest of your motion, so making a mistake here will likely sabotage the sections that follow. The main things to remember are to **make sure you turn on a flat—not steep—plane, and that you keep the clubhead outside your hands.**

TURN FLAT NOT STEEP

Don't make the mistake of moving your left shoulder toward your left foot. From this position, you'll swing down on the ball, not up. Instead, move it to the right while allowing it to work slightly down and under. (Iif you've been tilting, this will *feel* like a level turn.) Also, try turning your right hip away first. Not only will this keep your left shoulder in the correct position, but also increase the width of your swing (page 84).

SHIFT YOUR WEIGHT

Swing the club back and stop when your hands reach about thigh height. Remove your left hand from the grip and allow your left arm to hang straight down. If it hangs between your feet, then you've made a solid turn into your backswing. If it hangs near your left knee, then you've failed to get your weight turning into your right leg. You won't get much power from this position.

KEEP YOUR HAND POSITION

If your hands maintain their distance from your body during the takeaway, the clubhead will correctly stay outside your hands. If you allow them to pop out, your left arm and your hands will over-rotate, resulting in a laid-off position at the top. Feel like your body turn is leading your hands in the backswing and that your hands are leading the clubhead.

Bad turn with a reverse weight shift.

Solid turn with a solid weight shift.

HOW TO CHECK YOUR SHOULDER TURN

Lay your driver across your shoulders as shown and make your backswing. If you do it correctly, the shaft of your driver should sit perpendicular to your spine (picture a line from your chin to your belly button). If you make the typical mistake of turning too steeply while failing to shift your weight, the shaft will be almost perpendicular to the ground instead of to your spine.

NO
Shaft nearly perpendicular to the ground.

YES
Shaft perpendicular to spine angle established at address.

YOUR BASIC
DRIVER TOP POSITION

Don't lose control at the top—copy the moves here so you're in position to deliver the club with power.

As you motion the club to the top of your backswing, you need to prep for a move that will allow you to deliver the club back down to the ball from slightly inside the target line and with a powerful, *ascending* blow. Getting your right shoulder deep behind you and your left wrist flat at the top is critical. You'll also need to maintain a level elbow height and a strong right leg. Copy the positions you see here.

Right shoulder deep, left arm across chest.

1. FLAT LEFT WRIST
If your grip is solid and your left wrist is flat, then the clubface will sit at about a 45-degree angle at the top. If it's any more open than this (as when you cup your left wrist), you'll risk an open clubface at impact.

2. LEVEL ELBOWS
Your elbows should be nearly level, with the club sitting neatly between them. This indicates that you didn't over-rotate your left arm in your backswing. Nail this position and you'll have a much easier time squaring the clubface at impact.

3. STRONG RIGHT LEG
Your right leg should be fairly straight, but not locked and rigid. At the same time, your right hip should be a bit higher than your left, which will provide enough rotation for your right shoulder to get to the desired deep position.

4. DEEP RIGHT SHOULDER
As you finish your coil, make sure that your right shoulder is deep behind you (use your right ear as a guide), with your right elbow bent and your left arm across your chest. You'll need to nail this position to correctly deliver the club from inside the target line.

DEEP RIGHT SHOULDER: WHY IT'S SO IMPORTANT

Ideally, you should swing your driver as it travels below your waist on both sides of the ball on a path that mimics the lie of the club when you sole it on the ground (about 45 degrees). To deliver the club to the ball on this angle during your downswing, you need to start from what I like to call a "deep" position at the top (opposite page, bottom left). In other words, the clubhead needs to start its approach from near your body, not away from it. If you don't get your right shoulder deep enough on your backswing, the club will swing under your right shoulder on the downswing, making it difficult to hit the ball with a square clubface.

A SWING THOUGHT FOR GETTING DEEP

Feel like you're throwing a football at the tee from the top of your backswing. To do this, you have to pull your right shoulder way from the target and get your right arm bent and under the pigskin before you start your throw. If you don't get your right shoulder deep enough, your right arm can't move under the football. You'll miss the tee and you won't throw it very hard.

NO

If you tilt instead of turn, you'll over-rotate your left arm and bend your left wrist.

HURL A JAVELIN UNDERHAND

Here's a great way to sense what a power-rich inside delivery feels like from a deep position at the top. Hold your driver about three-quarters up the shaft (at its balance point) with your right hand and make a right-arm-only backswing. The club should be in line with your right forearm at the top. Start your downswing with the butt of the club moving toward the ball, and then as you shift your weight and begin to unwind, let the butt of the club point at the target. At impact, throw the club like you're throwing a dart (butt first). If you do it correctly the club should fly straight like a dart and not rotate like a helicopter.

Club in line with your right forearm.

Start down by pointing the butt at the target line.

As you continue to unwind, get the shaft moving down the target line.

Do it correctly and you should be able to throw the club at the target.

YOUR BASIC
DRIVER DOWNSWING

Creating lag and hitting the ball on the upswing are musts.

Coiled and deep at the top.

Arms swing as hips (*yellow circle*) stay still.

Same upper body rotation as Step 2.

DRILL: SWING, SLIDE, AND TURN FOR IMPACT

This drill will teach you how to separate your arm swing from your hip slide and torso turn in the downswing. **What you'll learn is that your arms play a more active role when hitting a driver.**

STEP 1
Get into a solid position at the top of your backswing and hold it. Make sure that your weight is firmly on your right side, your left wrist is flat and your elbows are level.

STEP 2
Slowly—*slowly*—swing your hands, arms, and the club down toward the ball on an arc.

STEP 3
While keeping your original upper body tilt and your back facing the target, continue to slowly swing your hands, arms and club down. Don't slide your hips forward just yet.

NOTES ON ARM SWING

It takes significantly more arm swing than you might think to make the club bottom out in the right place and strike the ball on the upswing, but you must swing your arms without losing your torso tilt. Notice in the drill below how my upper body is angled away from the target as I reach impact. This is mandatory to hit up into the ball and launch it high.

Hips slide forward (dashed line now closer to the ball).

Body stops. Arms pick up the pace.

Arms swing and torso turns into impact.

STEP 4
Begin to slide your lower body toward the target as your hips rotate to square (belt parallel to target line). You still want to keep your back facing the target as much as possible here.

STEP 5
Slide your hips into their impact position while turning them slightly toward the target. As you do this, swing the clubhead down to the ground at a spot just behind your left foot.

STEP 6
Swing the clubhead up into impact with your arms and with the grip end of the club slightly ahead of the clubface. Even though your chest and hips are turning toward the target, keep your head back.

YOUR BASIC
DRIVER THROUGH-SWING

Working on correct movements after impact can help you create correct movements leading up to it.

Believe it or not, a sound, powerful release and through-swing, in which you keep your head behind the ball and your tailbone in front of it, is about as important as any other part of your motion. **As you swing the club through the ball, keeping your hips forward and your head back preserves the upward angle of attack and clubface rotation you need to blast it high and deep.** Think about how you'd position your body if I asked you to throw your driver at the target. This will help you achieve maximum speed and solid contact.

 YES

In the release your left shoulder should be up and back, your right arm and right wrist should be fully extended and the clubface should be starting to roll clockwise so that the toe is more in line with the clubshaft. A good checkpoint is that a line drawn from your tailbone to the base of your neck leans noticeably away from the target. Notice here how my weight has transferred to my left foot, so much so that the left side of my body is a straight line.

HEAD BACK
Your head remains behind your tailbone even this late into the swing.

 NO

In an effort to speed up the clubhead and square the clubface, many golfers back their hips up and actually move them *away* from the target. This error immediately destroys your spine tilt, causing you to tilt toward the target instead of away from it. Moreover, it slows down the clubhead and negates the uprward angle of attack, with pop-ips and shots that start quickly to the left the typical results.

HANG BACK
Sure, my head is behind my tailbone, but most of my weight is on my right leg. Not good.

Video lessons on how to hit your drives longer and straighter at **golf.com/power** and on the tablet editions of Golf Magazine

POINT THE SHAFT

Choke down on the club and swing to just short of parallel with the ground (*photo, left*). If you correctly rotated your left arm, your elbow will be pointing downward and the shaft will point right of the target.

NO

If your left arm and elbow under-rotate you'll have a "chicken wing," with your left elbow and the butt of the club pointing well left of the target. This is a great move to produce a consistent slice.

Shaft pointed right of your target.

A PERFECT FINISH

Ending your driver swing in balance and with the club on the proper plane are signs of long-ball success.

In a proper finish the butt end of the club should point to the right of the target until the shaft gets parallel to the ground, at which point the butt should aim at the target. Rotating your left arm and bending your left arm correctly should make this easy to do.

Although the ball is long gone by the time you've reached the finish, you'd be surprised how much effect it can have on the overall quality of your shots. A poor finish is a clear indication of a poor swing, and vice versa. In order to hit the ball with power, and with some right-to-left movement, you must keep your left elbow in close to your body and your right arm fully extended. The drill at right shows you how.

PART 2: MAXIMIZING YOUR WOODS

Off the turf or off the tee. Here's how to crush your lofted metals.

The longest, largest-headed clubs with the least amount of loft you'll ever hit off the ground are fairway woods. Because of these factors you'll face unique challenges trying to make clean contact while taking full advantage of the true loft of the club. **The quick way to make easy work of powerfully sweeping shots hit with your fairway woods off the turf is to bottom out your swing in the correct place.** The keys you need to focus on are hitting the ball with a straighter, flatter path than what you use when hitting your driver, and not trying to hit the ball on the upswing.

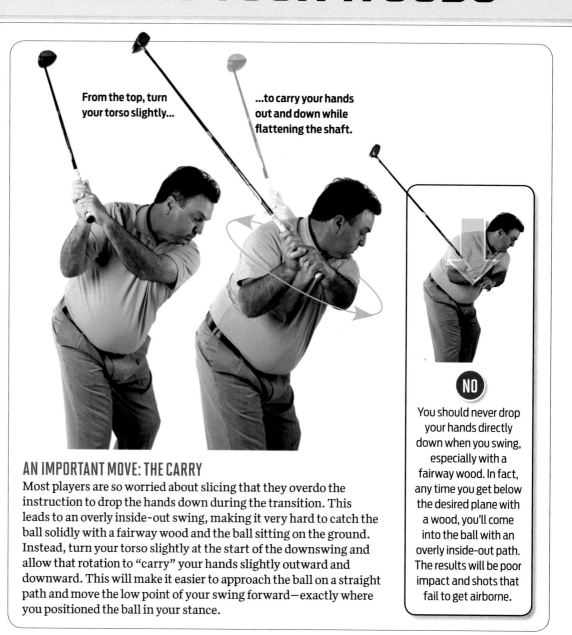

From the top, turn your torso slightly...

...to carry your hands out and down while flattening the shaft.

NO

You should never drop your hands directly down when you swing, especially with a fairway wood. In fact, any time you get below the desired plane with a wood, you'll come into the ball with an overly inside-out path. The results will be poor impact and shots that fail to get airborne.

AN IMPORTANT MOVE: THE CARRY

Most players are so worried about slicing that they overdo the instruction to drop the hands down during the transition. This leads to an overly inside-out swing, making it very hard to catch the ball solidly with a fairway wood and the ball sitting on the ground. Instead, turn your torso slightly at the start of the downswing and allow that rotation to "carry" your hands slightly outward and downward. This will make it easier to approach the ball on a straight path and move the low point of your swing forward—exactly where you positioned the ball in your stance.

NAIL YOUR SEQUENCE FOR SOLID CONTACT

Through impact you want your hips to lead your chest, your chest to lead your hands and your hands to lead the clubhead. Get this right and your angle of attack will be nice and shallow with your swing bottoming out in the correct place.

Outside of right shoulder inside the right foot.

Club in line with the left arm.

Chest slightly less open than the hips.

Hips well open.

YES

Your left shoulder should be nice and high at impact—feel a good stretch along the entire left side of your body.

NO

Here you can see my left shoulder isn't as high and my hips not nearly as open. These positions sap speed and power through the impact zone.

HOW TO MAKE A
POWER SWEEP

You must carve a straight path for solid shots.

The shape of your fairway woods and their relative lack of loft require that you swing on a straighter path to the ball than with irons or even your driver. Because you're trying to hit a rather large club off the ground, there just isn't as much leeway for an angled attack on the ball as with your other clubs. The key is to keep the clubface square to the arc of your swing for a longer period of time instead of allowing it to close quickly.

To preserve the clubface rotation you need to hit your fairway woods flush, it's critical that you get your left shoulder higher than your right through impact, and your left elbow higher than your right elbow. These positions might sound like a good way to slice the ball, but in reality they're what you want.

Another key move is to work your right hand under your left hand when the butt of the club is pointing at your belt buckle. Normally you'd like to have your right hand on top of your left in order to get the toe of the clubhead to pass the heel, but in this instance that's exactly what you don't want. Think "swing straight at the back of the ball" and then "swing to the left without the face turning over" and you'll have the right idea.

Swing less inside-out and more down the line through impact and you'll have an easier time sweeping the ball off the turf with a wood.

RIGHT HAND UNDER
Try to keep your right hand under your left through impact and beyond. You don't want to over-rotate the clubface when hitting a fairway wood.

IMPACT PATH: FAIRWAY WOOD VS. DRIVER

When hitting a fairway you want to swing more down the line and on a slightly descending path (about three degrees). You get this by having your chest and hips more open at impact, compared to when you're hitting a driver. Here's an easy way to distinguish between the two swings: you tilt more and turn less with a driver, and title less and turn more when hitting a fairway wood.

STRAIGHT PATH
You can clearly see how the path of a fairway wood swing is quite straight as it moves through the ball and into the release. This is critical for making solid impact off the ground.

ARCING PATH
The ideal path for a driver is significantly more round and arcing. The driver is hit off a tee and should move much more inside-to-out through impact.

FAIRWAY WOOD: The clubhead should descend slightly into the ball on about a three-degree angle.

DRIVER: In contrast, a driver should ascend through the ball on an approximately five-degree angle.

PART 3:
MAXIMIZING YOUR HYBRIDS

Your best friend on the course requires a few slight adjustments to pay dividends.

Hybrids are designed with a much lower center of gravity than long irons and are much easier to hit. However, they require a swing that has a relatively shallow angle of attack, meaning the ball needs to be struck much closer to the bottom of the swing arc for them to work properly. **The best way to do this is with a swing dominated by loose arms and wrists.** I recommend practicing off a low tee with the goal of just barely clipping the tee without making much contact with the ground.

COMBO CLUB
Unlike the upward swing you use with a driver or the downward swing you use with your irons, you make contact with a hybrid near the bottom of your swing with a sweeping motion.

Swing your arms back while shifting your weight onto your right foot...

...change directions...

...and swing your arms through while shifting your weight onto your left foot.

SWING YOUR HYBRIDS WITH YOUR ARMS

To get the feel of the swing action that works best with hybrids, get into your setup without a club and with your palms facing each other, about six inches apart. Make sure your arms are hanging down naturally with no stiffness.

Start swinging them back and forth with your weight shifting to your right and left foot as you swing your arms left and right, respectively. As you do this, think, "Right foot backswing, left foot downswing" and you'll get the idea. While you're swinging back and forth like this, imitate good moves by flattening your left wrist and bending your right at the top and then reaching impact with slightly less right wrist bend and a more noticeably bowed left wrist.

> ## "THEY REQUIRE A SWING THAT HAS A RELATIVELY SHALLOW ANGLE OF ATTACK."

HOW TO
DOMINATE OFF THE TEE

Ten ways to get the most from your swing before pulling the trigger.

1. EVALUATE THE HOLE, the landing area, weather conditions, etc., and how to fit a shot you're are likely to hit into the plan.

2. PICTURE THE SHOT you want to hit and make any practice swings needed to feel the mechanics to pull it off.

3. SEE A LINE heading in the direction you need to aim at to execute the shot. This might be very different than the target line.

4. USE A SPOT or an area to assist you in maintaining your aim while transitioning from behind the ball to when you start stepping in.

5. STEP IN with your right foot first as you line the club up. You should have your forward bend and

1 EVALUATE
Survey the hole ahead of you and select an appropriate landing spot and a swing that will get you there.

2 SEE THE LINE
Focus on the direction you need to aim as you transition from facing the target to facing the target line.

Video lessons on how to hit your drives longer and straighter at
golf.com/power *and on the tablet editions of* Golf Magazine

distance from the ball set by now.

6. ALIGN YOUR BODY to the club by stepping in with your left foot. Widen your right foot to set your stance width. Face forward, not toward the ball.

7. WAGGLE THE CLUB using your wrists and bend your right arm with each waggle. Get a feel for the club's weight.

8. LOOK DOWN THE LINE where you're aiming one last time and follow that line back to the ball by swiveling your head.

9. BREATHE—inhale and exhale one last time.

10. START your swing with a small weight shift to the left (a mini-step) before shifting to the right as you take the club away.

WAGGLE TIP
Don't just use your wrists. Bend your right arm so you waggle the club on plane.

3 STEP IN
Go right foot first and then left when building your stance, all the while focusing on your target.

4 RELAX
Take one last breath to clear your mind and waggle the club to get a feel for the weight of the club.

YOUR SHORT GAME: CHIPS, PITCHES & LOBS

You don't need every shot in the book to be a savvy short-game player, just three reliable ones. Here's how to hit them and get up and down from anywhere around the green.

A GAME OF
THREE KEY SHORT SHOTS

INSIDE
Three ways to learn
the basics you need:

LESSONS
Tips and instruction
to help you master
fundamental moves
and positions

CHECKPOINTS
Tests to see if you're
keeping up or falling
behind in your quest to
build a better game

DRILLS
Practice tips and
step-by-step exercises
to make new moves
second nature

Nailing the three basic short shots will transform your game and your handicap.

t's safe to say that the short game isn't the sexiest part of golf. Big drives, par-5-destroying hybrids and laser-like iron shots tend to be more exciting to most players than pitching and chipping, but the fact remains that **if you want to be a solid player who shoots good scores (and shoots them consistently), then you must develop a reliable short-game technique .**

All you need to look at for proof of this fact is the telecast of any PGA Tour event, particularly on Sunday afternoon. The guys who are in contention are the players getting the ball up and down consistently, while those who fall apart give away bogeys and worse every time they miss a green. Think of it this way: the average PGA Tour player hits about 65 percent of his greens in regulation, meaning he has to deal with at least six missed greens every round. Therefore, a good short game can save six strokes per round, while a poor one can cost six. Now how many strokes per round would that mean to you?

In this chapter I'll teach you everything you need to know about three basic shots—the chip, pitch and lob—that will allow you to handle just about any situation within 30 yards of the green. Once you learn how to set up properly, swing correctly and then sharpen those skills, all you'll have to do when faced with a short shot on the course is ask yourself if you have more green to use or more trouble to avoid and you'll know the correct shot choice.

THE BASIC SHORT SHOTS

Chip: A short shot from near the green hit with your less-lofted wedges and all the way down to your 8-iron. It's a tiny stroke—more like what you use when putting than what you use for a pitch or full-swing shot.

Pitch: A less-than-full shot normally used from 10 to 50 yards from the green and with your most-lofted wedges (sand wedge for a medium trajectory and lob wedge for a higher trajectory).

Lob: A high-lofted pitch that spends almost all of its time in the air and rolls a very short distance.

> "A GOOD SHORT GAME CAN SAVE SIX STROKES PER ROUND, WHILE A POOR ONE CAN COST SIX."

YOUR SHORT GAME GURU

GOLF
MAGAZINE
TOP 100
TEACHERS
IN AMERICA

JASON CARBONE
Baltusrol Golf Club,
Springfield, N.J.
Golf Magazine Top 100 Teacher (2007–present)
● *Top 40 Teachers Under 40* (2007)
● *Best Young Teachers* (2010)
● Teaching since 1993
golf.com/instruction

PART 1:
YOUR BASIC CHIP SHOT

When you have room in front of you and no trouble to carry, this shot is always the highest-percentage choice.

There are a lot of shots you need to know to be a complete golfer, but the basic chip is one you absolutely must have to play at any level. Just like a get-it-in-play tee shot, mid-iron shot from the fairway or short putt, the basic, rolling chip will come into play every single time you tee it up. You can't hide from it, so you have to learn it sooner or later. I suggest making it sooner.

A chip shot is used only when there's a decent amount of green between you and the hole with very little—if any—trouble to go over. The shot plays basically like a long putt, hitting the green quickly and then rolling the majority of the way to the target. Once you learn the basic setup and swing, which is dominated by the arms and upper body, **the key is to approach these shots almost the same way you would a putt.** Picking your target line and reading the green to determine break and speed will be critical to your success.

ADDRESS
A very basic setup that allows your arms to hang directly beneath your shoulders with a choked-down grip and your eyes inside the ball.

BACKSWING
Your shoulders control your arms, hands and club as they move into an abbreviated backswing. No need for a ton of wrist hinge here.

NOTES ON STANCE

When you set up to hit a chip shot, stand close enough to the ball so that you remove any angle in the top of your left wrist. **Check that your left thumb and forearm are directly in line.** This sets your club on a more upright lie and encourages a less-arcing swing, both of which are good for developing greater accuracy. Chipping with more of a straight-back-and-through motion is the easiest way to contact the ball before hitting the turf and guard against catching the ground early and chunking the shot.

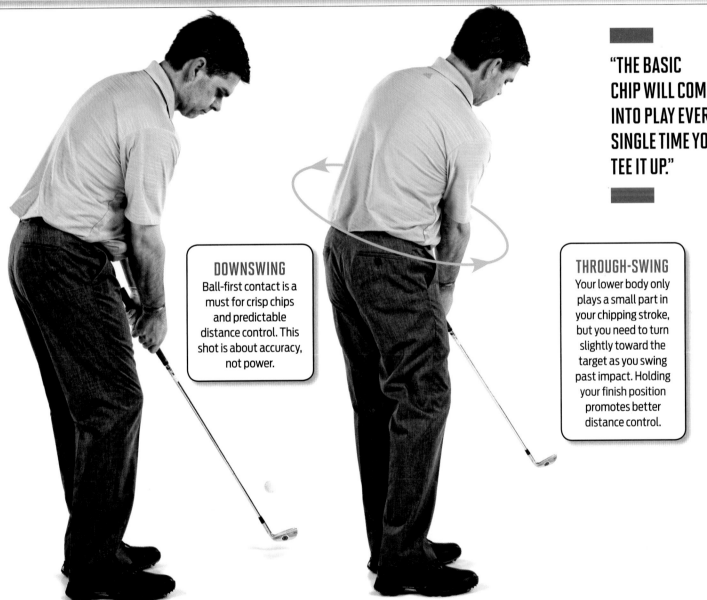

"THE BASIC CHIP WILL COME INTO PLAY EVERY SINGLE TIME YOU TEE IT UP."

DOWNSWING

Ball-first contact is a must for crisp chips and predictable distance control. This shot is about accuracy, not power.

THROUGH-SWING

Your lower body only plays a small part in your chipping stroke, but you need to turn slightly toward the target as you swing past impact. Holding your finish position promotes better distance control.

HOW TO NAIL YOUR
CHIP-SHOT SETUP

Keeping it simple is the key to good chipping. Think small when it comes to stance and grip and you'll be headed in the right direction.

A s is the case with any shot in golf, a proper setup is critical for solid chipping. One of the most common mistakes I see among recreational players on these relatively simple shots is putting themselves in a position to fail before they even make a swing. Placing the ball too far forward or back leads to inconsistent contact. Stances that are too wide or too narrow and gripping the club too high on the handle make distance control more difficult than it needs to be. The basics outlined here, which give you the correct stance width, grip and ball position, are really all you need to worry about before you get into the swing. Nail these every time and you'll be in good shape to move forward.

1 STANCE WIDTH

To get your stance width correct, you need to think small, but not too narrow. Don't make the mistake of putting your feet completely together, as I see many players do. Instead, place your feet so they're about two clubheads apart. This should feel a bit narrower than your normal stance, where your feet are basically under the insides of your shoulders. Your left foot should be open a bit (rotated toward the target), while your right foot should be square to the target line.

FEET

You want your feet fairly close together, but not too close. Think about the width of two clubheads and you'll be in the right neighborhood.

2 GRIP

The proper grip for chip shots is really no different from your normal grip. Where you take your grip on the handle, however, should be significantly different. For a full shot with a driver, for example, you want to hit the ball high and long, so you grip the handle all the way at the end. This promotes maximum clubhead speed, height and distance but sometimes at the expense of accuracy and control. For a chip shot you want the opposite result, so you need to grip the club down near where the rubber ends. Gripping down allows you to stand closer to the ball and trace a swing path that leads to consistent contact and better accuracy. This position will feel a bit different at first, but with some practice you should get comfortable quickly.

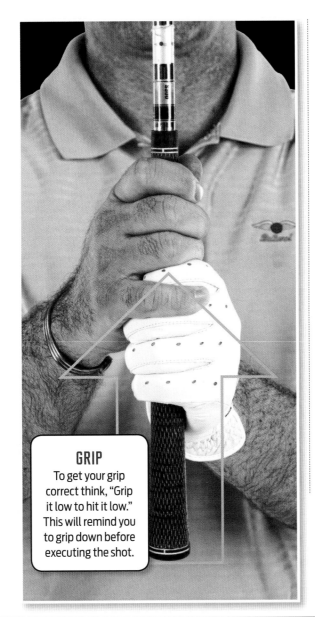

GRIP
To get your grip correct think, "Grip it low to hit it low." This will remind you to grip down before executing the shot.

3 BALL POSITION

You want this shot to fly a very short distance and roll most of the way to your target. Remember, this shot is almost like a long putt except that you're hitting it with an iron rather than a putter. To promote the maximum amount of roll, position the ball directly under your right ear. If this is hard to figure out you can also use the instep of your right foot as a guide. This position will make it easy to strike the ball cleanly before your club touches the ground, and it will also minimize backspin while producing a very low trajectory. Don't get carried away and put the ball behind your ear or right instep, as this will make you much more likely to hit the shot fat or thin. Stick with the proper position and the shot is relatively simple.

BALL POSITION
Line a club up with your right ear— wherever the club points is where you should position the ball in your stance. Think "Right ear for rolling shot."

STEP-BY-STEP:
THE CHIP-SHOT SWING

This is a small shot that requires a small swing. It's all about control and creating a solid strike.

While there isn't a lot of wrist hinge required to hit a solid chip shot, you can't go at it with stone-hard hands. Just a little hinge is all you need to strike the ball with a slightly descending swing and accurately control your distance.

HOW TO DO IT

A great way to develop the correct chipping motion is to place a tee in the cap of the grip (*photo, near right*). At address, the tee should point at your left rib cage. When you take the club back (mostly by turning your shoulders), hinge your wrists a bit so the tee points at your left hip rather than your rib cage. This is all the wrist hinge you need, and you should feel only a slight bend in your right wrist.

Once you reach the point where the tee is pointing at your left hip, stop your backswing and swing down to the ball. Do it by turning your chest and stomach toward the target and dropping the clubhead onto the ball while keeping the tee pointed at your left hip the entire time. **As long as you keep your grip pressure constant, you'll eliminate the chance of decelerating or even over-accelerating when you swing.**

CHECKPOINT 1

At address you want the tee to point directly at your left rib cage. This will put your hands, arms and club in the proper position. Make sure you get this right every single time.

CHECKPOINT 2

In the takeaway, hinge your wrists just enough so the tee points at your left hip. This ensures that you have the proper amount of wrist hinge to strike the ball with a descending blow. Don't allow the tee to point below your hip.

CHECKPOINT 3

As you swing through impact, be certain that the tee continues to point at your left hip. This will create the proper amount of release through the shot and help you strike it solidly and with greater control.

Release or hold— it's up to you.

DON'T DO THIS

In the finish you should strive to maintain your balance with both feet comfortably flat on the ground. More importantly, keep the tee pointing at your front hip. The common mistake is to swing the clubhead to high like I'm doing here. Make sure the clubhead is low to the ground in your finish.

EASY WAYS TO
PRACTICE YOUR CHIPPING

Learn to rotate your torso in harmony with the club to hit solid chip shots every time.

In order to hit solid chip shots consistently it's critical to create a downward strike on the ball. To do so you not only have to have a bit of wrist hinge in your motion (*see page 106*), but you must also pivot your upper body in harmony with the club. You should feel like your arms are connected to your chest and simply turn your body. This is a lot easier to do and more reliable than trying to hit the ball only with your arms and hands.

The key to being successful with this move is to point your shirt buttons at the grip of the club at all times during the swing. Here are three drills to give you all the right feels.

CHART YOUR PROGRESS

How to Hit the Key Short Shots	☑ Chip-shot technique
	❑ Pitch-shot technique
	❑ Lob-shot technique
	❑ Swing fine-tuning

DRILL NO. 1:
TURN TO 11 O'CLOCK

Place a club across your shoulders so it's parallel to the target line, or just a bit open, at address. Picture a clock face on the ground around you. At address the grip of the club should be pointing to 12 o'clock (*photo, right*).

Once you're set, turn your torso to the left so the clubshaft moves from 12 o'clock to 11 o'clock on the dial. Do this repeatedly until you get the feeling of this move. This is all the turn you'll need to hit a solid chip.

ADDRESS
Set the shaft at 12:00.

THROUGH-SWING
Set the shaft at 11:00.

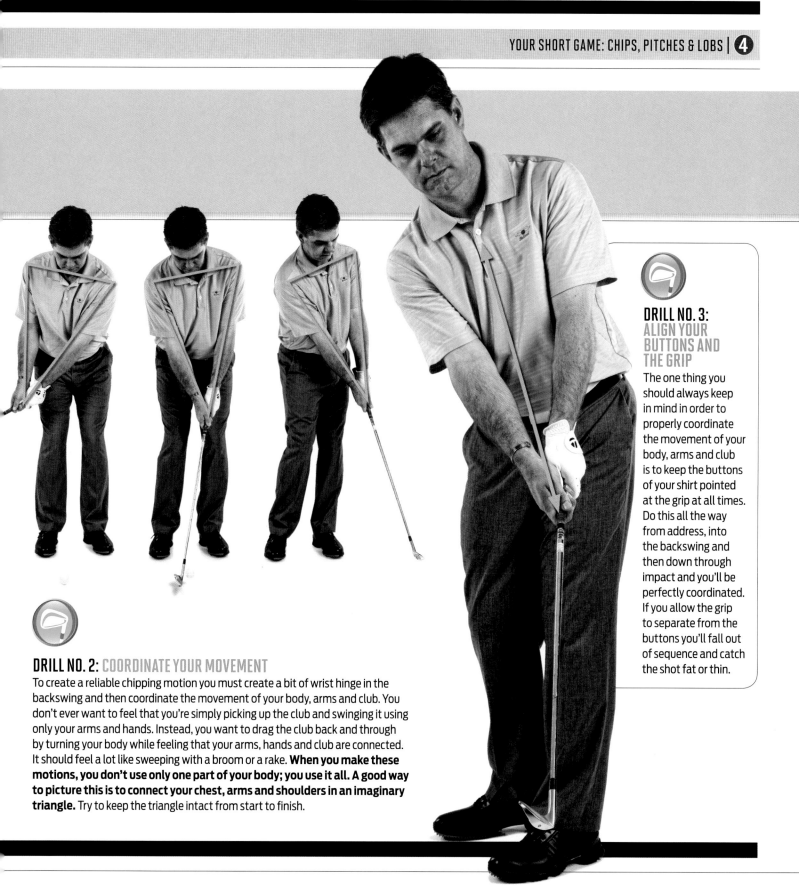

DRILL NO. 3: ALIGN YOUR BUTTONS AND THE GRIP

The one thing you should always keep in mind in order to properly coordinate the movement of your body, arms and club is to keep the buttons of your shirt pointed at the grip at all times. Do this all the way from address, into the backswing and then down through impact and you'll be perfectly coordinated. If you allow the grip to separate from the buttons you'll fall out of sequence and catch the shot fat or thin.

DRILL NO. 2: COORDINATE YOUR MOVEMENT

To create a reliable chipping motion you must create a bit of wrist hinge in the backswing and then coordinate the movement of your body, arms and club. You don't ever want to feel that you're simply picking up the club and swinging it using only your arms and hands. Instead, you want to drag the club back and through by turning your body while feeling that your arms, hands and club are connected. It should feel a lot like sweeping with a broom or a rake. **When you make these motions, you don't use only one part of your body; you use it all. A good way to picture this is to connect your chest, arms and shoulders in an imaginary triangle.** Try to keep the triangle intact from start to finish.

PART 2:
YOUR BASIC PITCH SHOT

When you have some trouble to fly over and less distance between the edge of the green and the hole, this shot is the best option.

Like the basic chip, the basic pitch is a shot you'll need every time you play. Anytime you miss a green you'll be faced with choices, and having a reliable pitch shot in your arsenal will prove invaluable time and again. **The pitch shot is only slightly different from the chip in terms of setup, but the resulting ball flight can be significantly different.**

A pitch shot is used when there's trouble or a good amount of fairway or rough between you and the hole. Unlike a chip, which rolls almost the entire distance to the hole, a pitch shot spends more time in the air, up to 70 percent of the total distance. This isn't a shot you use to clear a gaping bunker with the flag just on the other side, but you can use it to clear smaller bunkers, rough, sprinkler heads or any other type of trouble between you and the hole.

BACKSWING
Use significantly more wrist hinge than with the chip shot, and a longer backswing. This shot needs to get into the air and fly most of the way to the hole.

ADDRESS
The basic pitch setup is very similar to a chip shot setup except that you set your hands at the end of the grip instead of near the steel. This will promote the correct downward strike and a more-lofted shot.

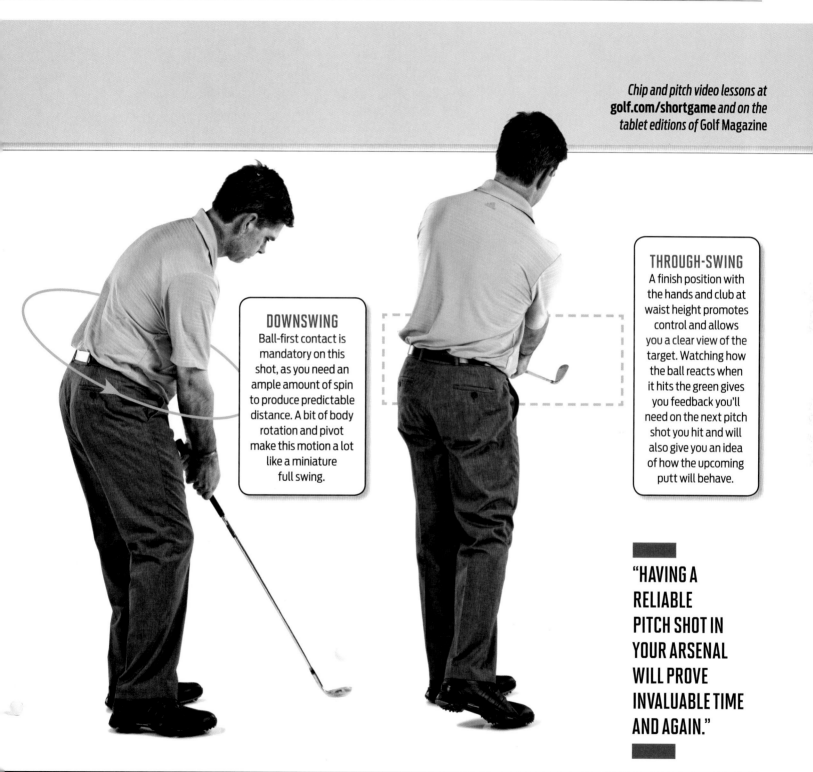

Chip and pitch video lessons at **golf.com/shortgame** *and on the tablet editions of* Golf Magazine

DOWNSWING

Ball-first contact is mandatory on this shot, as you need an ample amount of spin to produce predictable distance. A bit of body rotation and pivot make this motion a lot like a miniature full swing.

THROUGH-SWING

A finish position with the hands and club at waist height promotes control and allows you a clear view of the target. Watching how the ball reacts when it hits the green gives you feedback you'll need on the next pitch shot you hit and will also give you an idea of how the upcoming putt will behave.

"HAVING A RELIABLE PITCH SHOT IN YOUR ARSENAL WILL PROVE INVALUABLE TIME AND AGAIN."

HOW TO NAIL YOUR
PITCH-SHOT SETUP

You want to create some loft when pitching, which demands a longer grip and a more forward ball position.

Like all shots in golf, the pitch shot requires a proper setup in order to strike the ball solidly and produce the desired amount of loft, spin and distance. **In comparison with the chip-shot setup, the pitch shot requires a more forward ball position** and a slightly wider stance. Also, you'll need to grip the club closer to the end of the handle rather than near the metal. Learn the basics outlined here (which give you the correct stance width, grip and ball position) and you'll have everything you need to hit a proper pitch shot every time.

1 STANCE WIDTH

The proper stance is relatively narrow, about three clubheads, but not so narrow that you feel off balance. You want to feel athletic and relaxed, with your weight equally distributed between your feet, or a bit more over your front foot. Your right foot should be square to the target line, with your front foot a bit open (toe pointed more toward the target). You want to be comfortable and feel that you can drop the clubhead on the ball without losing your footing.

FEET

Don't make the mistake of placing your feet too close together. The width of three clubheads is a good guideline, but feel free to experiment a bit if this doesn't feel comfortable.

2 GRIP

You should use the same grip for a pitch shot that you use for a normal shot, meaning that unlike with the chip shot, your hands should be placed more toward the end of the handle of the club. This grip placement effectively makes the club longer, which promotes a longer swing, more wrist hinge and shots with a bit more loft. Don't make the mistake of holding the club right on the butt of the grip—you're not trying to hit home runs like Babe Ruth. Make sure the very end of the grip is visible after you take your hold and you should be in a good position.

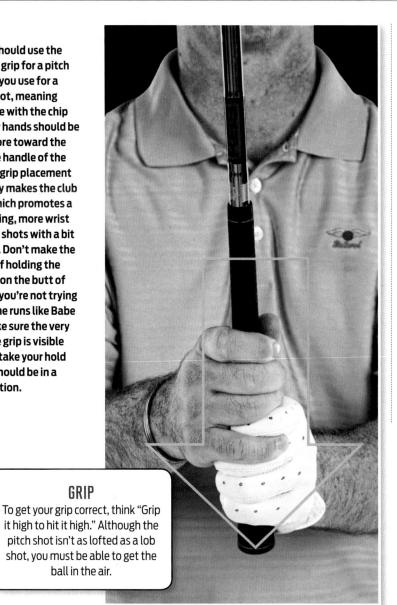

GRIP

To get your grip correct, think "Grip it high to hit it high." Although the pitch shot isn't as lofted as a lob shot, you must be able to get the ball in the air.

3 BALL POSITION

The pitch shot needs to get into the air and fly a significant way to the hole. To promote more loft you need to position the ball under your left ear, which is quite a bit more forward than you would with a chip shot (under your right ear). This more forward position will increase loft at impact and will make it much easier to pop the ball into the air. Don't make the mistake of playing the ball too far forward or you'll find it very difficult to hit it solidly. Instead, the result will be inconsistent contact and less spin.

BALL POSITION

Line a club up with your left ear—where the club points is where you should position the ball in your stance. Don't play the ball any more forward than this. Think "Left ear for lofted shot."

STEP-BY-STEP:
THE PITCH-SHOT SWING

Extra wrist hinge and a slightly longer swing are key to producing the loft and spin you need to get it close to the hole.

The pitch swing requires more folding of the right arm as the club moves away from the ball, and a bit more hinging of your left wrist. **This combination of moves will put the club in a position to strike the ball with a slightly downward swing,** which is critical to producing the necessary amount of loft and spin. On the way back down to the ball, use the same moves that make your full swing work, the most important being turning through the ball so that your body is facing the target in your finish.

CHECKPOINT 1
Start with the butt of the club pointing just to the left of your belt buckle. Your arms should have a solid structure and support the club, but not be tight or tense.

CHECKPOINT 2
Rotate your shoulders to take the club into the backswing, and stop when your hands reach waist height. You should allow your right elbow to fold a bit and your left wrist to hinge. The shaft of the club should be close to parallel to the ground, but it's okay to go a bit higher. At this point, your left shoulder should clearly be below your right.

CHECKPOINT 3
Use your turn to swing the club down and through into a balanced finish with your body facing the target and the club out in front of you. Focus on you body pivot—excess hand and arm action on your downswing won't give you the descending, ball-first strike you need to pitch it crisp.

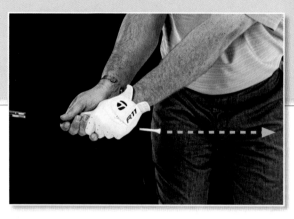

DRILL NO. 1:
HINGE AND TURN

To get a feel for the right kind of wrist-hinge action you need to hit a solid pitch, try the following:

STEP 1

Take your pitch address position with the club soled on the ground. Once you're set, hinge the club up in front of you using only your wrists. Hinge it to the point where the shaft is parallel to the ground and the toe of the clubhead points straight up.

STEP 2

Without moving anything else (especially your wrists), rotate your upper body to the right until the clubshaft is both parallel to the ground and to your target line. This is where you need to be each and every time you pitch.

DRILL NO. 2:
POINT THE TEE

It's all you need to pull together all the keys for a solid motion.

STEP 1

Place a tee in the end of the grip (*photo, below*) and take your address. Make sure the tee is pointed just left of your belt buckle. This sets your hands in the proper position to take the club away with the correct amount of wrist hinge and elbow break. If the tee points to the right side of your belt buckle, then you've added unnecessary loft to the clubface.

STEP 2

As you take the club back, the tee should remain hidden under your left forearm. Continue your swing by hinging your right elbow and your wrists until the club reaches parallel to the ground. A great checkpoint here is that the tee points parallel to your target line.

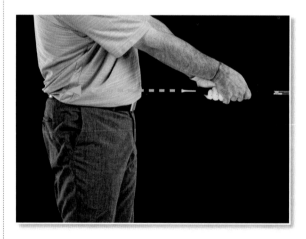

STEP 3

At impact, the tee should again be pointing just left of your belt buckle. But don't stop there. Continue turning your body through the shot so that, at your finish, the tee points at your belt buckle. Notice in the photo above how the shaft of the club is parallel to the ground—this will maximize your control of the shot and promote a proper release. You also want to make sure that your chest and belt buckle are facing the target.

EASY WAYS TO
PRACTICE YOUR PITCHING

"Shake hands" on both sides of the ball to groove the proper motion for pitching it clean.

In order to hit good pitch shots, you need to extend your right arm down your toe line on both sides of the ball. In the backswing, your right elbow should bend slightly and your right wrist should hinge a bit. In the follow-through, your right arm should be extended straight down your toe line, with your chest and belt buckle facing the target. **Imagine you're turning to shake hands with someone on your right as you take your backswing, then turning to shake hands with someone on your left in your follow-through. This will help you develop the proper feel**

Think of your pitch swing as a simple arcing motion, with your right arm swinging along the line of your toes. Rotate your body slightly going back and through to keep everything in sync.

CHART YOUR PROGRESS

How to Hit the Key Short Shots		
	☑	Chip-shot technique
	☑	Pitch-shot technique
	☐	Lob-shot technique
	☐	Swing fine-tuning

DRILL NO. 1:
SHAKE HANDS

This easy visualization allows you to groove the right kind of pitch turn.

STEP 1
Take your address position without a club in your hands. Imagine that two of your friends are standing on your toe line on both sides of the ball, directly facing you. To replicate a solid backswing, extend your right arm with a slightly bent elbow as if you were shaking hands with the friend on your right. Don't make a big body turn. Use mostly your right arm to reach out to your buddy.

BACKSWING
In the backswing you want your right arm pointing down your toe line but with a slightly bent elbow. Move your arm by slightly opening your right shoulder, but don't turn your entire torso.

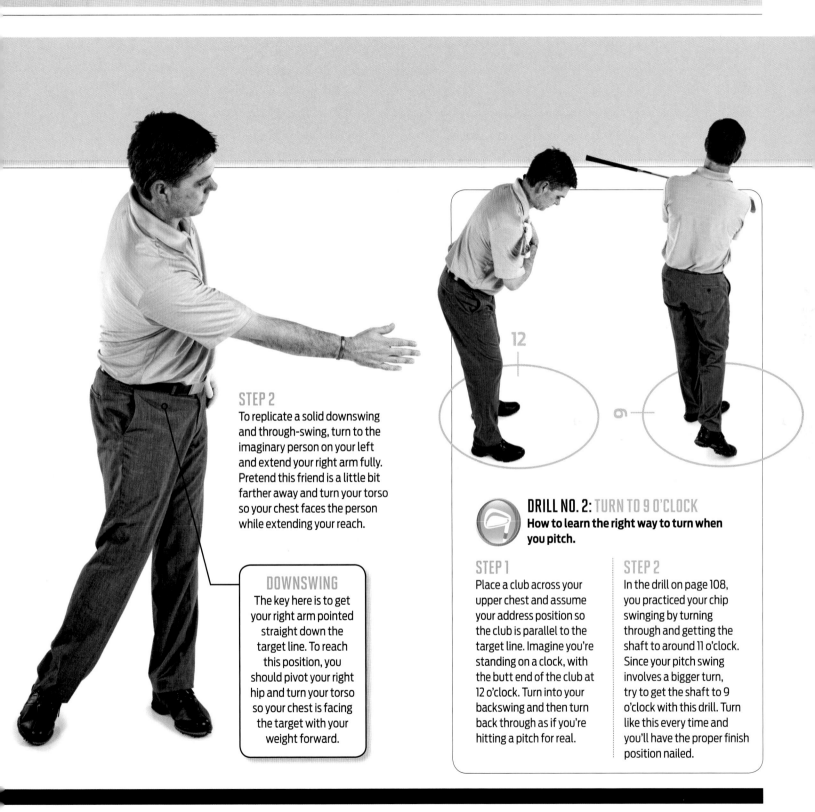

12

9

STEP 2

To replicate a solid downswing and through-swing, turn to the imaginary person on your left and extend your right arm fully. Pretend this friend is a little bit farther away and turn your torso so your chest faces the person while extending your reach.

DOWNSWING

The key here is to get your right arm pointed straight down the target line. To reach this position, you should pivot your right hip and turn your torso so your chest is facing the target with your weight forward.

DRILL NO. 2: TURN TO 9 O'CLOCK
How to learn the right way to turn when you pitch.

STEP 1

Place a club across your upper chest and assume your address position so the club is parallel to the target line. Imagine you're standing on a clock, with the butt end of the club at 12 o'clock. Turn into your backswing and then turn back through as if you're hitting a pitch for real.

STEP 2

In the drill on page 108, you practiced your chip swinging by turning through and getting the shaft to around 11 o'clock. Since your pitch swing involves a bigger turn, try to get the shaft to 9 o'clock with this drill. Turn like this every time and you'll have the proper finish position nailed.

PART 3:
YOUR BASIC LOB SHOT

When you have serious trouble to get over and very little green to work with, this is the shot you'll need.

Of all the short-game shots you'll face, the lob requires the steepest swing in order to produce an immediate, high trajectory and plenty of shot-stopping spin. You use it when there's trouble between you and the hole, like a big, deep bunker or thick rough, and you have little room between the edge of the green and the flagstick. As you'll soon learn, generating the loft, spin and softness you need mandates a unique setup.

During the lob swing it's critical to hinge your wrists so the club is pointing straight up at the sky when your left arm is parallel to the ground in your backswing. You'll need to create this angle if you want to get the ball high enough into the air. Another important aspect of the lob swing is sliding your knees slightly toward the target on your downswing. **The idea is to slide the clubhead under the ball to create maximum loft.**

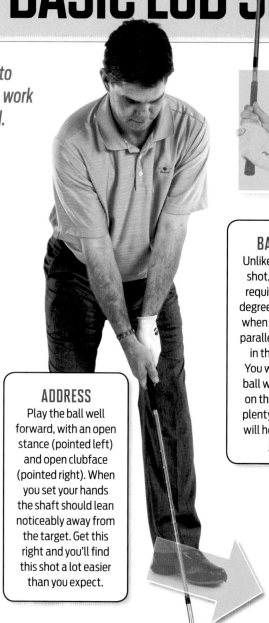

ADDRESS
Play the ball well forward, with an open stance (pointed left) and open clubface (pointed right). When you set your hands the shaft should lean noticeably away from the target. Get this right and you'll find this shot a lot easier than you expect.

BACKSWING
Unlike a chip or pitch shot, the lob swing requires at least 90 degrees of wrist hinge when your left arm is parallel to the ground in the backswing. You want to get the ball way up in the air on these shots, and plenty of wrist hinge will help you get the job done.

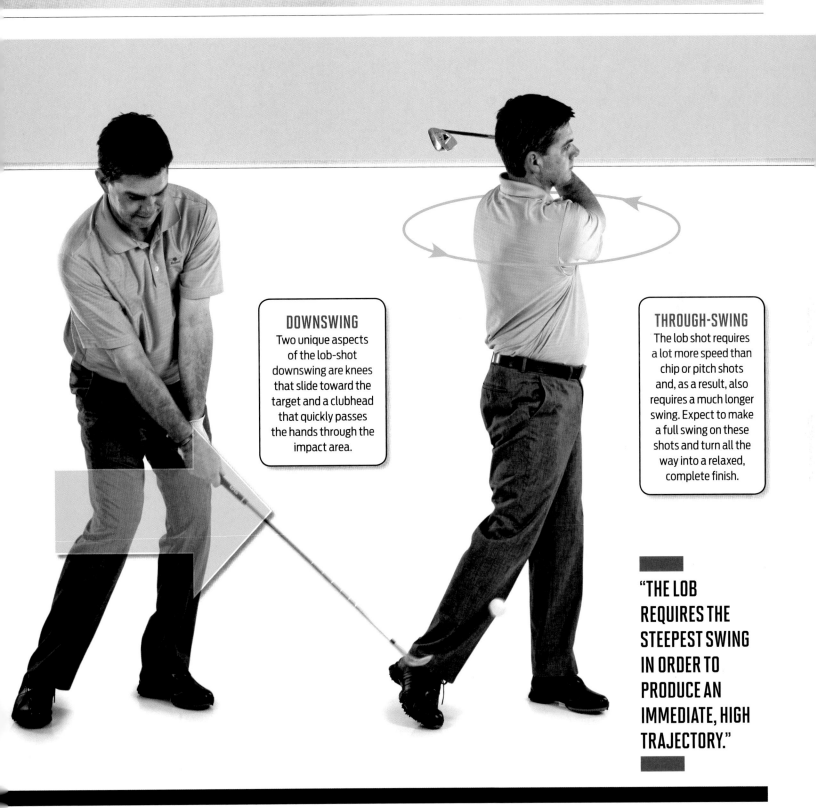

DOWNSWING
Two unique aspects of the lob-shot downswing are knees that slide toward the target and a clubhead that quickly passes the hands through the impact area.

THROUGH-SWING
The lob shot requires a lot more speed than chip or pitch shots and, as a result, also requires a much longer swing. Expect to make a full swing on these shots and turn all the way into a relaxed, complete finish.

"THE LOB REQUIRES THE STEEPEST SWING IN ORDER TO PRODUCE AN IMMEDIATE, HIGH TRAJECTORY."

HOW TO NAIL YOUR
LOB-SHOT SETUP

The lob is a specialty shot and requires a unique setup. Get the keys right and you'll find this shot easier than you expect.

The lob is a unique shot that calls for a setup that's more extreme than you'll find in most situations. The goal of the lob is to loft the ball high into the air and get it to land softly, safely flying over whatever serious trouble sits between you and the flagstick. Though it might seem like an intimidating shot, if you nail the proper setup you'll likely find it less difficult than you expected. The points you need to get correct are a wide stance that's open to the target, a clubface that's open and a ball position that's off your left shoulder. **All these adjustments will encourage the club to slide under the ball with a slightly open face, creating plenty of loft and a steep angle of descent near your target.**

1 STANCE WIDTH

You need a wide stance to execute an effective lob shot. The width of your shoulders is a pretty good guide, which is fairly similar to what you would use for a normal full swing. You also want your stance to be a bit open, with your left foot pulled back away from the ball so that the toe is in line with the heel of your right foot. This adjustment will also open your shoulders (pointing to the left of the target), making it easier for you to swing the club to the left through impact and brush the grass under the ball. It will also allow you to maintain the extra loft you created at address.

2 BALL POSITION

In golf, the more forward you play the ball, the higher it will typically go. On this shot you want the ball to go almost straight up, so you need to position the ball off your left shoulder, which is also close to even with your left toe. To check this spot, take your address position and hold the grip of your wedge against your left shoulder so the club hangs straight down. Where the club points is where you want to play the ball. Even if this spot feels too far forward, stick with it.

3 CLUBFACE

Unlike most other shots in golf, the lob requires a clubface that's open at address and at impact, meaning it is pointing slightly right of the target, a position that actually adds a bit of loft and makes it easier to hit the ball high into the air. If you take your setup and then simply rotate the grip of the club clockwise in your hands just a bit and then regrip the club, you should easily find the correct clubface position.

STEP-BY-STEP:
THE LOB-SHOT SWING

Swing along your foot line with plenty of wrist hinge and you'll create all the loft you need.

The lob swing requires the greatest amount of wrist hinge, the longest backswing, the most speed and the steepest plane. All of these factors combine to create a very high-flying shot that both goes up and comes down steeply. **Though it looks different from a chip or pitch swing, it shouldn't be much more difficult to execute once you understand the technique.** Check the key positions at right to make sure you're in the right place at the right time.

CHECKPOINT 1
This shot works best with a lob wedge—if you don't have one, get one. The extra loft and shorter shaft length will help you make a steeper swing and create the loft you need at impact to launch the ball high.

CHECKPOINT 2
As you swing through impact, keep your arms and hands nice and loose. Soft hands allow your wrists to unhinge easily, a critical move that slides the clubhead under the ball so it can pop the ball up.

CHECKPOINT 3
To make a solid lob swing, you have to set up properly and then swing along your foot line. It will feel like you're swinging to your left, or across the ball, but this is mostly because your body is aiming to the left.

Video lessons on how to hit the perfect lob shot at
golf.com/shortgame *and on the tablet editions of Golf Magazine*

LOOK IN THE FACE

To see if you're going at it correctly, make your lob swing and stop the club at about chest height after you pass through the impact zone. If you've released the clubhead properly, the clubface should be looking straight at you. (If it had a mirror on it you'd see your eyes in the reflection.) If you're having trouble creating this position, try "throwing" the clubhead through impact so it passes your hands before they get to the ball. You should quickly be able to see the clubface as you reach chest height. This move is critical for creating loft and height on the shot.

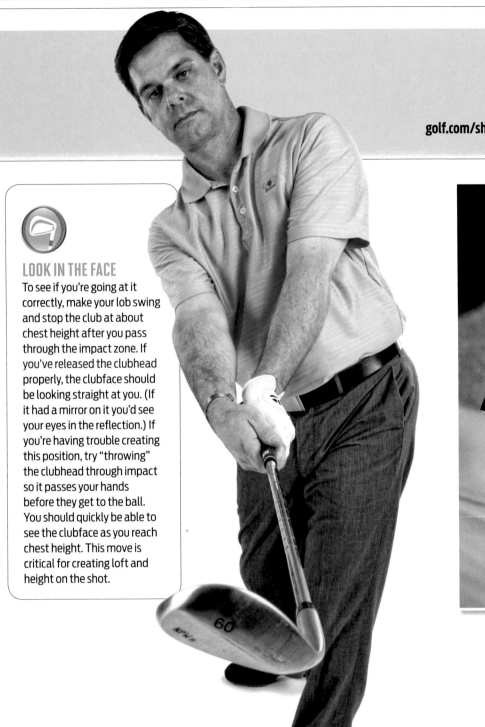

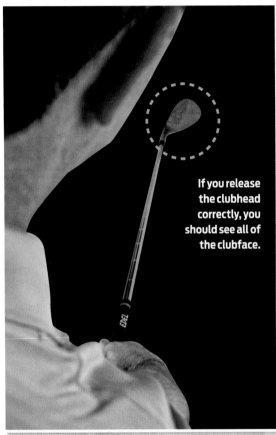

If you release the clubhead correctly, you should see all of the clubface.

CHART YOUR PROGRESS

How to Hit the Key Short Shots	☑ Chip-shot technique
	☑ Pitch-shot technique
	☑ Lob-shot technique
	☐ Swing fine-tuning

PART 4:
FINE-TUNE YOUR SHORT GAME

You now know how to get it close. Next up: how to get it closer.

N ow that you have the basics down, it's time to take your short game to the next level by tweaking it here and there to make sure you have the right shot for the situation you're facing. **Good short-game players know how to dial in distance and trajectory as if turning on a light switch.** I'll show you some easy ways to adjust ball flight on the fly, as well as to add spin and get out of the most common short-game lies out there. I'll finish by clueing you in on how to select the right set of wedges and get the specs you need to take advantage of your swing and the conditions in which you typically play.

A DRILL FOR DISTANCE
One of the things you'll have to do once you have your technique down is figure out what club typically provides the best results for you. Club selection for most short-game shots, including chipping, is a matter of personal preference, and finding the wedge that produces the most consistent, controlled shots is the final step to perfecting your results around the green. Here's an easy way to find out which club will be your go-to choice for chipping.

> **STEP 1**
> Find a good chipping spot on the edge of a level practice green. Place one club on the green about 3 yards away and another club about 12 yards away.

ROLL THE BALL ALL THE WAY
TO THE SECOND CLUB

**CARRY THE BALL
OVER THE FIRST CLUB**

3 YARDS

9 YARDS

STEP 4
Once you find the club that gives you the most consistent 1:3 ratio, adapt it to different shot lengths by making a longer or shorter swing, but stay true to the carry-to-roll values (*see chart below*). Then, vary the trajectory, finding the club that gives you the best 1:1, 1:2, 1:4, etc., ratio by adjusting the drill at left.

STEP 3
Closely monitor your results that each club until you find the one that's easiest for you to control and which provides the most consistent results. Keep in mind that the ultimate idea is to find a club that can fly the ball 25 percent of the way to the target and roll it the remaining 75 percent of the total distance.

STEP 2
Try chipping balls with your 8-iron, 9-iron, pitching wedge and sand wedge, landing each ball over the near club while trying to stop each one at the far club.

NAIL YOUR DISTANCES

1/4 CARRY DISTANCE	3/4 ROLL DISTANCE	TOTAL DISTANCE
3 yds.	9 yds.	12 yds.
4 yds.	12 yds.	16 yds.
5 yds.	15 yds.	20 yds.
6 yds.	18 yds.	24 yds.
7 yds.	21 yds.	28 yds.
8 yds.	24 yds.	32 yds.
9 yds.	27 yds.	36 yds.
10 yds.	30 yds.	40 yds.

MAKE YOUR PITCHES
RUN OUT OR STOP

Perfect your pitching by improving your touch and expanding your shot selection.

Although a pitch shot is one that normally flies at least halfway to the hole, there are variations that you need to have in your arsenal in order to shoot your best scores. **The two main types of pitch shots that I suggest you get familiar with are the runner and the spinner.** The former is used when you need the ball to release and roll over a tier or up a slope, while the latter is used when you need to minimize roll and get the ball to stop as quickly as possible. A good way to think of these two shots is by the type of release you need to execute with each. To make the ball run when it hits the green you must release the toe of the club through impact; to make it spin, you must prevent it from turning over.

HOW TO HIT A RUNNING PITCH

To get the ball to run the majority of the distance to the hole, you must allow the toe of the club to rotate over the heel as it passes through impact (This means you must let it release.) At the finish the toe should point up at the sky and the heel at the ground. This rotation of the clubface helps create a bit of draw spin and will send the ball rolling a lot like a putt when it hits the green.

HOW TO HIT A SPINNING PITCH

To carry the ball most of the way and get it to stop quickly when it hits the green, you must prevent the toe of the club from passing the heel through impact. The easy way to do it is by retaining the angle of your right wrist all the way through the shot (This means holding off your release.) You did it correctly if the clubface is at about a 45-degree angle in your finish.

FEEL YOUR DISTANCES

The main goal of every short-game shot is fairly clear: get the ball as close to the hole as possible. To do so, the critical component is obviously controlling the distance the ball travels after you hit it. While this may sound relatively easy (like throwing horseshoes or playing boccie), it takes quite a bit of practice to truly get the feel of pitching a ball a specific distance.

To quickly and easily develop your distance control and feel, pick a target (preferably on a practice green) and simply **toss balls underhand to the hole.** For targets that are farther away, you'll have to make your arm swing longer, and for shorter targets you'll make it shorter. Also, try varying the amount of loft you create for each toss, sometimes getting the ball well into the air and sometimes almost bowling it to the hole. After a while you'll start to see where the appropriate landing spots are for given distances and begin to get adept at hitting them. Once you reach this level, pick up your wedge and try to hit the same spots using actual swings.

Feel like you're tossing a ball toward the ground to hit a lower shot.

Feel like you're tossing a ball high to hit a higher shot.

PITCH IT TIGHT
FROM FAIRWAY OR ROUGH

Handle tight lies and rough with some simple alterations to your swing.

In order to pitch the ball effectively on a consistent basis, **you have to be able to deal with standard lies as well as two other common trouble lies:** those that are very tight (little grass under the ball), and those that are very thick (lots of heavy grass around the ball). Regardless of where you play most of your golf, you'll likely find your ball sitting in both situations from time to time, and knowing how to handle them will be critical. Here's all you need to know.

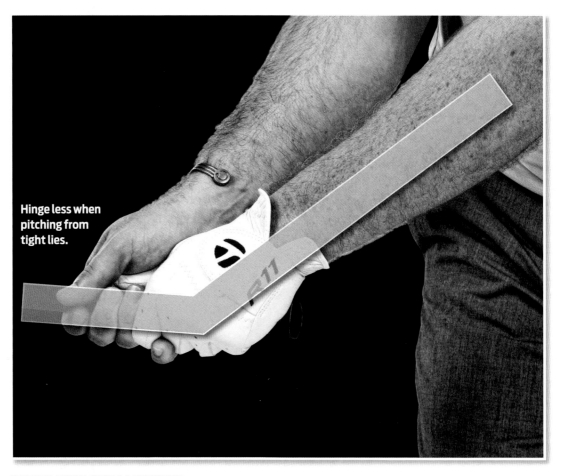

Hinge less when pitching from tight lies.

HOW TO PITCH FROM A TIGHT LIE

When you have a very tight lie, **hinge your wrists a bit less in the backswing and make your swing a bit wider.** The key is to clip the ball cleanly by making sure you contact the ball before you hit the ground. To promote a clean hit, play the ball under your sternum. This provides ample margin for error by exposing the bounce of the club and making it less likely that the leading edge will dig into the turf.

Hinge more when pitching from rough.

HOW TO PITCH FROM THE ROUGH

When faced with a lie in thick rough, **hinge your wrists more than normal and make a slightly narrower swing.** The key is to drop the clubhead down onto the ball so you can get through the thick grass surrounding it and pop it out onto the green. These shots can be a bit tricky and they often come out with very little shot-stopping spin. Take this extra roll into account when planning where to land the ball on the green.

BUILD A STEEP SWING TO ESCAPE TALL GRASS

A good way to ingrain the proper feel of a pitch from the rough is to place a head cover about a foot to the right of the ball and try to hinge your wrists up sharply enough to miss the head cover but still hit the ball. This will teach you to take the club up and back on a very steep angle, which is mandatory for shots from thick rough.

FINE-TUNE YOUR
WEDGE SET MAKEUP

Putting the right kind of wedges in your bag is almost as important as learning the right technique.

There are a number of things you need to get right with your wedges in order to make them perform the best for your swing. The first thing you should do is make sure you have an appropriate range of lofts to accommodate the variety of distances you'll face on the course. **Typically it's best to space your set four to six degrees from wedge to wedge,** meaning if you have a 48-degree pitching wedge you'd ideally also have a 52-degree gap wedge, a 56-degree sand wedge and a 60-degree lob wedge. However, many modern iron sets now have 45-degree pitching wedges, which means you'll need a 50-degree gap wedge, 55-degree sand wedge and so on.

GET IN TOUCH WITH BOUNCE

Almost more important than loft, however, is bounce angle. This design trait has a tremendous effect on how a wedge interacts with the turf during a shot. Bounce is your margin for error. If you have the correct amount of bounce on your wedges, the bottom of your swing doesn't have to be perfect and you'll basically eliminate balded and chunked short shots from your game. If you were to error on one side, use wedges with too much bounce, but your best option is to go through a custom fitting so you can start taking advantage of this very important club specification.

I put impact tape on the soles of three wedges with three different bounce angles. Markings on the tape indicate where the club made contact with the ground. This contact point is the key to determining if your clubs have too much or too little bounce.

NO

NOT ENOUGH BOUNCE

The mark on this wedge shows it has too little bounce. Notice how almost no tape has been scuffed off the sole of the club and that the mark is all the way to the front of the leading edge. This club will dig into the ground excessively and be very hard to hit.

What wedges to buy, the specs you need and information on all of the latest designs from the major manufacturers at golf.com/equipment

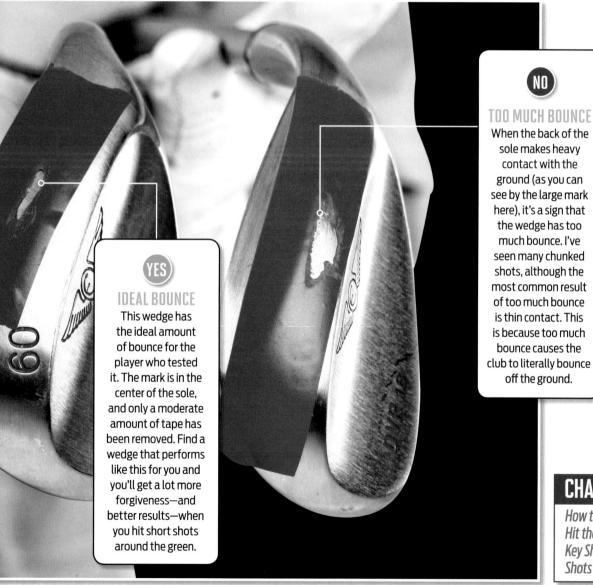

NO

TOO MUCH BOUNCE

When the back of the sole makes heavy contact with the ground (as you can see by the large mark here), it's a sign that the wedge has too much bounce. I've seen many chunked shots, although the most common result of too much bounce is thin contact. This is because too much bounce causes the club to literally bounce off the ground.

YES

IDEAL BOUNCE

This wedge has the ideal amount of bounce for the player who tested it. The mark is in the center of the sole, and only a moderate amount of tape has been removed. Find a wedge that performs like this for you and you'll get a lot more forgiveness—and better results—when you hit short shots around the green.

"IF YOU HAVE THE CORRECT AMOUNT OF BOUNCE ON YOUR WEDGES, THE BOTTOM OF YOUR SWING DOESN'T HAVE TO BE PERFECT."

CHART YOUR PROGRESS

How to Hit the Key Short Shots	☑ Chip-shot technique
	☑ Pitch-shot technique
	☑ Lob-shot technique
	☑ Swing fine-tuning

SIX STEPS TO PERFECT PUTTING

How to read the green, pick your line, make your stroke and drop the ball
in the hole using a simple plan that makes putting seem easy

HOW TO MAKE
MORE PUTTS

INSIDE
Three ways to learn
the basics you need:

LESSONS
Tips and instruction
to help you master
fundamental moves
and positions

CHECKPOINTS
Tests to see if you're
keeping up or falling
behind in your quest to
build a better game

DRILLS
Practice tips and
step-by-step exercises
to make new moves
second nature

Putting is a challenging part of the game. You can only master it if every part of your green technique is in full working order.

By the time you reached two years old you could already communicate ideas—albeit simple ones—like, "Juice, Mommy" and "Uppy, Daddy." The ideas themselves weren't as significant as the fact that you could actually speak, or the process you used to learn how to communicate, which was to focus on the big picture first and simply find a way to get words out of your mouth. Only later did you get around to learning the details that support communication: letters, words, grammar, etc.

Fast-forward 15 years, to the time when you tried to learn a second language in high school. There, you took the opposite approach, focusing on the mechanics of grammar first while cramming to memorize words and tenses. What became of that effort? You probably failed to master the language and now can only spout off a few words and phrases.

The way you learned how to speak as an infant is the way you should learn how to putt—by focusing on the big picture first. **Taking this route, instead of focusing on the little things first like you did when you tried to learn a second language, keeps you from getting bogged down in mechanical details that, while relevant, aren't the essence of good putting.**

I strongly suggest that you work on this chapter in the order presented. You'll begin by defining or refining your putting process (*pages 138–141*) and then move on to the next section, which outlines how to assess your skills (*pages 142–167*). At that point, you'll be in a great position to consider the details within your technique—the "grammar" portion of making putts.

THE PUTTING PROCESS
You need the following to become a great putter:

1. Green Reading: Judging slope and speed and the predicted roll of the ball from start to finish.
2. Speed Control: Using a stroke that matches the distance needed to roll the ball to the hole.

"THE WAY YOU LEARNED HOW TO SPEAK AS AN INFANT IS THE WAY YOU SHOULD LEARN HOW TO PUTT."

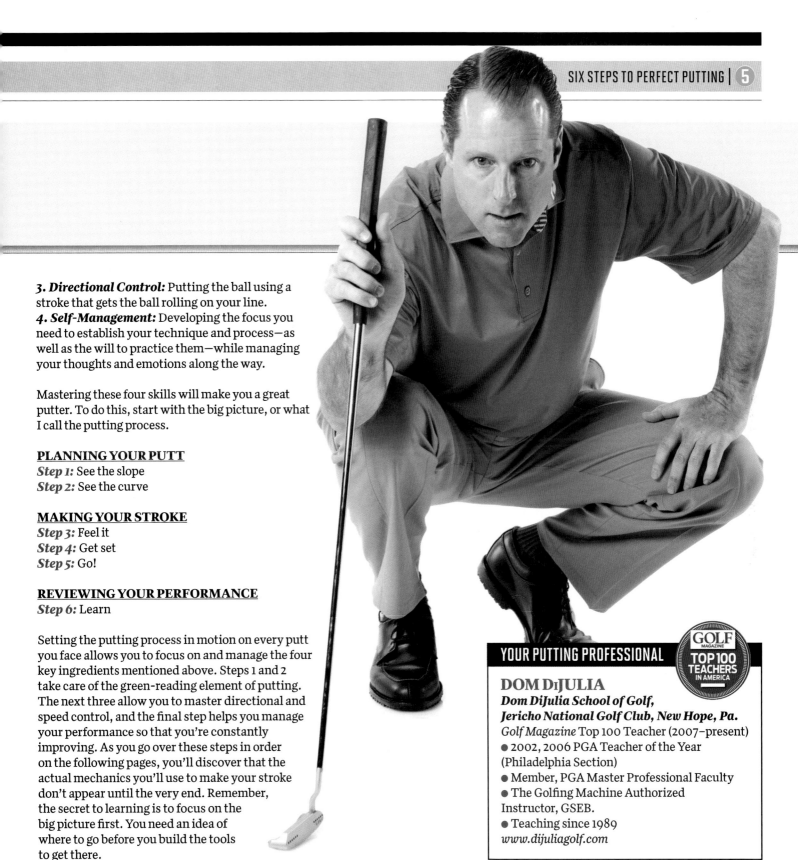

3. Directional Control: Putting the ball using a stroke that gets the ball rolling on your line.

4. Self-Management: Developing the focus you need to establish your technique and process—as well as the will to practice them—while managing your thoughts and emotions along the way.

Mastering these four skills will make you a great putter. To do this, start with the big picture, or what I call the putting process.

PLANNING YOUR PUTT
Step 1: See the slope
Step 2: See the curve

MAKING YOUR STROKE
Step 3: Feel it
Step 4: Get set
Step 5: Go!

REVIEWING YOUR PERFORMANCE
Step 6: Learn

Setting the putting process in motion on every putt you face allows you to focus on and manage the four key ingredients mentioned above. Steps 1 and 2 take care of the green-reading element of putting. The next three allow you to master directional and speed control, and the final step helps you manage your performance so that you're constantly improving. As you go over these steps in order on the following pages, you'll discover that the actual mechanics you'll use to make your stroke don't appear until the very end. Remember, the secret to learning is to focus on the big picture first. You need an idea of where to go before you build the tools to get there.

YOUR PUTTING PROFESSIONAL

GOLF MAGAZINE TOP 100 TEACHERS IN AMERICA

DOM DiJULIA
Dom DiJulia School of Golf,
Jericho National Golf Club, New Hope, Pa.
Golf Magazine Top 100 Teacher (2007–present)
● 2002, 2006 PGA Teacher of the Year (Philadelphia Section)
● Member, PGA Master Professional Faculty
● The Golfing Machine Authorized Instructor, GSEB.
● Teaching since 1989
www.dijuliagolf.com

HOW TO PLAN
THE PERFECT PUTT

The first things to do when devising a plan of attack are to see what you're putting over and how it will affect the ball's roll.

STEP 1: SEE THE SLOPE

Every green is sloped, and sometimes these slopes are significant. Learning to see them clearly is the first step when facing any putt. Start out by carefully surveying the ground you're putting across and the green as a whole. Forget about the length of your putt for the moment and focus solely on slope. In our junior camps, we successfully get five-year-olds to "see the hill." While this suggestion seems simple and obvious, my years of teaching have convinced me that 95 percent of recreational players fail to do it and begin planning their putts before truly identifying the nuances of the green and the hill(s) these putts will encounter.

HOW TO DO IT

To properly assess slope you have to get in position to actually see it. I know some of you look at putts from both sides of the hole and that you probably think this covers all of the bases from a green-reading perspective, but I bet you're more confused after looking at the green from the

second spot than you were after looking at it from the first. That's because you see things differently depending on the point from which you look. **Therein lies the key to nailing step 1 of the putting process—look at the green and see the hill from the right spot.**

I'll make things easy on you here: find the low point on the green and assess the slope from there. This gives you the best perspective on the size and shape of the hill(s) in general and, more importantly, relative to your line of putt. Of course, there are a slew of technical reasons why this is the case, but I won't bore you with geometry and ocular science. Just take my advice and survey the green from its lowest point, and do it on every putt. Consistency is key. Once you start varying your vantage point (either from hole to hole or from round to round), you'll start confusing your eyes and make hill assessment more difficult than it is. Plus, if you try to survey the hill from any other spot on or near the green, you'll only be engaging in guesswork, and that's not going to cut it.

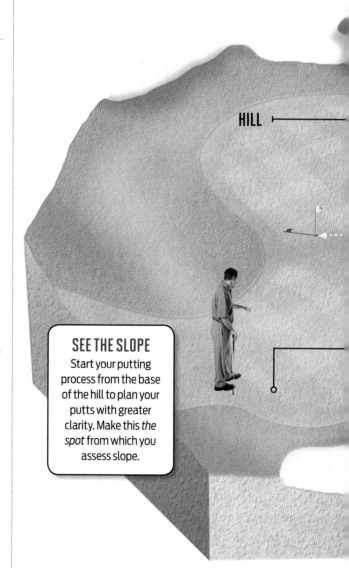

HILL

SEE THE SLOPE
Start your putting process from the base of the hill to plan your putts with greater clarity. Make this *the spot* from which you assess slope.

"TRY DOING A BIT OF 'MONKEY SEE, MONKEY DO' WITH THE BEST PUTTER YOU KNOW."

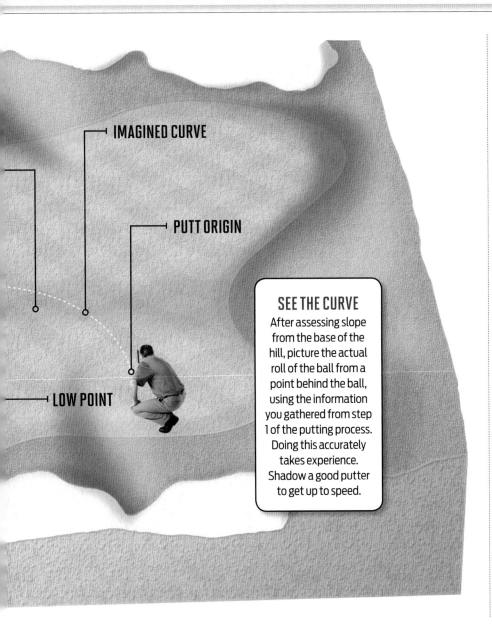

IMAGINED CURVE

PUTT ORIGIN

LOW POINT

SEE THE CURVE

After assessing slope from the base of the hill, picture the actual roll of the ball from a point behind the ball, using the information you gathered from step 1 of the putting process. Doing this accurately takes experience. Shadow a good putter to get up to speed.

STEP 2: SEE THE CURVE

Now that you've seen the hill, you can begin imagining how it's going to affect the ball's roll. Seeing the roll in your mind's eye is the key in this step of the putting process.

HOW TO DO IT

If you're like most players, you see an accurate curve for less than half of your putts. More importantly, your imagination and experience aren't developed enough to give you even a puncher's chance of making anything outside of six feet. Don't sweat it, because that's about to change. Check out the quote below from a student of mine. I think it provides a winning solution to your visualization problems:

"If you want to learn how to visualize putts, stand behind a good player and watch him or her putt from down the line."

This student could see hills and slopes correctly, but was unable to either bring up the right picture or aim in the direction he intended. So I lined up and stroked putts with him watching me from down the line, and then had him immediately step in and copy what he saw. His putting improved markedly and immediately. This showed that he could aim where he wanted, but that his ability to imagine the curve of the ball was below par, especially on the extreme hills that we were putting over.

Try doing a bit of "monkey see, monkey do" with the best putter you know and you'll start visualizing putts a lot more accurately. Better yet, perform this drill on the course with your coach and your improvement will be even more dramatic. To really amp up your visualization skills, turn the page.

HOW TO
SEE CURVES LIKE A PRO

New ways to see the line and accurately picture the ball rolling into the hole.

ADVANCED VISUALIZATION

Picturing the ball's roll to the hole gives you a good idea of the curve you'll have to deal with. But your picture has to be razor sharp. Here's how to hone your curve-reading skills and predict putts like it's second nature.

Start by getting behind the ball and picturing its roll. As you do this, **move slightly from side to side without getting out of your posture** (*photos, right*). After a while, the curve will become quite obvious, and you'll see the roll in a whole new light.

DOWN TARGET
Look down the ball-to-hole line (*solid black line*). If your imagined roll of the putt (*dashed yellow line*) looks like it will miss to the left if it follows this line, then...

SLIDE
...move over to your left. Find the point where a line drawn from you through the ball will obviously start the ball too far out to the right. Then...

SLIDE AGAIN
...move back in between these two borders and look for the place that allows you to imagine the putt rolling directly away from you and into the hole. (Reverse the steps if the ball looks like it will miss to the right when you look down target.)

NOTES ON VISUALIZATION

Seeing the speed you think the ball will roll across the green is just as important to your success as seeing its direction. To get a better sense of speed, imagine that you're watching your putt on TV. Most players only imagine a curve or a line, which is a good start, but you should do it in a way that's more like watching a video rather than simply looking at a still photo.

LINEAR PUTTING

Some players prefer to see lines. If this is you, adjust your visualization to include a spot to putt toward instead of trying to get the ball rolling on a curve.

Putt to a spot both on your starting line and equidistant to the hole.

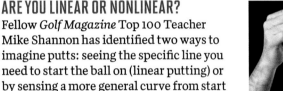

ARE YOU LINEAR OR NONLINEAR?

Fellow *Golf Magazine* Top 100 Teacher Mike Shannon has identified two ways to imagine putts: seeing the specific line you need to start the ball on (linear putting) or by sensing a more general curve from start to finish (nonlinear putting).

For you non-linear putters, move on to Step 3 of the Putting Process (page 140) since you've already learned what you need to know in order to picture the curve correctly. **For you linear putters, there are a few additional steps.**

Once you have your curve, picture a spot on your starting line that's as far away from you as is the actual hole (*photo, left*). Completing your visualization by locating this spot gives you perfect information on distance and direction and allows you to putt to a spot rather than along a curve.

If you want to get even more precise with your line, "draw" it on the ground using your puttershaft. You can plumb-bob the line or hold the shaft in front of your eyes.

Drawing a "T" on the ball can also enhance your ability to aim at your linear target. Simply point the base of the "T" at your spot and set the putterface parallel to the top of the "T" when you take your address. Doing this, however, mandates that you practice pointing the "T" accurately, otherwise you won't point it correctly when you play. And once you point it, you need the will to commit to your "T" line even when it doesn't feel right when you're standing over the ball.

Draw your line by plumb-bobbing...

...or hinging the shaft up.

Draw a "T" on the ball and point it down your starting line.

HOW TO GET A
FEEL FOR THE PUTT

How to move smoothly from reading your line to the actual act of putting while getting a feel for the right speed and distance.

Making a practice stroke while looking at the ball is good for checking mechanics.

Making a practice stroke while looking at the hole is good for gauging distance.

STEP 3: FEEL IT

You know which iron to pull from your bag to fly the ball onto the green from 100 yards with a standard swing (as well as the one to pull when you're 150 yards out, 180 yards out, 200 yards out—wherever). When you're on the green, however, these options disappear. The club you pull when you're facing a 50-foot uphill putt is the same one you grab when facing a slick, 10-foot downhiller (your putter in both cases). And whereas you rely on the length and loft of your irons and woods to control speed and distance from the tee box and fairway, **it's all up to you on the greens, because you're using the same club for every putt.** This is why step 3 of the putting process—getting a feel for speed and distance—is so critical to putting success.

HOW TO DO IT

Take a moment before each putt to determine the energy it will require to reach the cup. This is a vital step that only the most experienced and skilled players can skip. Get the right feel by making focused practice strokes and grooving a motion that promotes your ability to hit a solid putt. Make the first practice stroke to rehearse your mechanics (a technical practice stroke) and the second to dial into the speed of the putt you're facing (a feel practice stroke).

You can make your practice strokes while looking at the ball or at the hole. You can make continuous strokes or individual strokes. Regardless of your technique, the important thing is that you actually develop one and, even more critical, that you repeat it every time you putt without any deviations. Once you

USE TWO SETS OF PRACTICE STROKES
Make a practice stroke while looking at the ball to feel your technique, and then one while looking at the hole to develop your touch (with the feel of your technique still fresh in your mind).

develop your routine in this area (or any other), test it for at least 10 rounds and see how it works before considering a new method. Switching philosophies after every disappointing putting round is a great way to keep your handicap higher than it should be.

NOTES ON GETTING SET

If you're working on something specific in your setup (staying balanced, getting your eyes in the right place, etc.), feel free to perform a final scan of the fundamental as you perform step 4 of the putting process. (You'll learn a lot more about the setup on pages 158–165.)

STEP 4: GET SET

There's only one more thing to do before you start your stroke, and that is to simply step up to the ball and get set. **Accomplished players make this a smooth and flowing process by creating practical shortcuts.** One of these is moving from their practice strokes to the ball without completely re-creating their setup. There are two "walk-in" methods (*photos, right and below*) that get the job done nicely:

WALK IT IN, PUTTER FIRST
Move from your practice stroke to your setup by sliding your putter behind the ball, then walking your feet into your stance.

WALK IT IN, FEET FIRST
Move from your practice stroke to your setup by stepping your feet to the ball, then sliding the putterhead into position.

STEP 5: GO!

At this point you've checked off the list of things you need to do to ensure success. **The final task is to stroke the putt.**

If you nail steps 1–4, step 5 should be easy—just "go."

HOW TO DO IT

The easiest way to make a solid stroke, especially if you're an inexperienced golfer, is to simply execute a carbon copy of the practice strokes you made in step 3. If you're more of a seasoned player, your goal should be to pull the trigger and putt without thinking—to stroke the ball from your subconscious mind. The key is to trust your technique and the hours you've logged on the practice green—you're more than ready to make the putt.

Here are a few ways of leaping into the "go!" part of your process:

1. Look at your target. Look at the ball. Go.
2. Sense the speed of the putt and go.
3. Trust your plan, your distance and directional control and just try to hit a solid putt.
4. Trust your distance control and use a single swing thought for this putt ("tick-tock" or "head steady," for example).

THE LAST STEP:
REVIEWING YOUR RESULTS

The last step of the putting process involves learning from your mistakes so that you don't keep making them.

STEP 6: LEARN

If you're like most amateurs, you focus so much on the quality of your results that you fail to see what your results can teach you. That has to change. One of the fastest ways to start hitting better putts is to use a little objective observation during practice and play—watch how your putts roll and learn from what you see. In order to do this, you need to quiet the fan in you and stop rooting for yourself. **The fan could care less about learning; he just wants to see if the putt goes in or not.** If it doesn't, he mentally changes the channel, which eliminates the possibility for learning.

HOW TO DO IT

Stop rooting and pay attention! Ask yourself the questions at right after each and every putt. Doing so allows you to remain focused on developing the vital skills all great putters share without letting your emotions—or the fan in you—get in the way. Ask the questions in order, and if you're honest with your answers, you'll accelerate your learning faster than you ever thought possible.

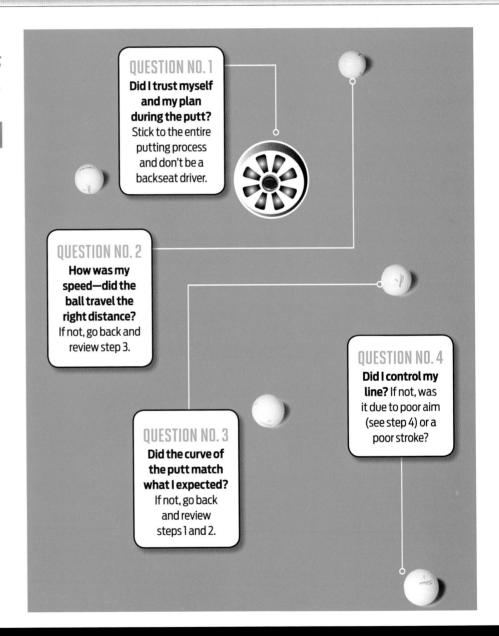

QUESTION NO. 1
Did I trust myself and my plan during the putt? Stick to the entire putting process and don't be a backseat driver.

QUESTION NO. 2
How was my speed—did the ball travel the right distance? If not, go back and review step 3.

QUESTION NO. 3
Did the curve of the putt match what I expected? If not, go back and review steps 1 and 2.

QUESTION NO. 4
Did I control my line? If not, was it due to poor aim (see step 4) or a poor stroke?

REVIEWING THE FOUR SKILLS

I've just covered all that you need to know to improve your green reading and pre-putt plan of attack. I've also shared some good ideas on how to self-manage and better control distance and direction. However, there are many other factors that affect these skills, and now is a good time to test them. I'm including a skills test before getting into the details of setting up and actually executing a stroke because you may be doing these things correctly already. Why fix something that isn't broken? Perform the tests at **golf.com/basicsbook** before applying any of the instruction on the following pages. Your putting stroke doesn't define your putting skill; it merely supports it.

AFTER THE TEST

If your results from the putting tests show that your mechanics need work, keep in mind that there isn't a single-best method or technique that you must employ to putt well. **Good putters have always gone about their business in vastly different ways because they know that the real goal is ball control, not stroke perfection.**

The photos at right show just 15 of the millions of ways to consistently roll the ball into the hole. While helping you discover the one that will work best for you, I'll suggest a few fundamentals on the following pages that apply to any successful stroke. Regardless of the path your putting journey takes, the most important thing you need to do to become a great putter is to define your method and dedicate yourself to mastering it.

Ball forward   Ball back   Norman-style   Nicklaus-style   Piston stroke

Hinge back   Hinge through   Saw grip   "Y" backstroke   "Y" through-stroke

Left hand low   Belly putter   Long putter   Left-side anchor   Long claw

STROKE BASICS NO. 1 & 2:
BALANCE AND PLANE

Make your stroke your own, but with an eye toward including the following putting-stroke basics.

BASIC NO. 1: STABILITY

You'll improve both your distance and directional control if you can keep unnecessary movement to a minimum and establish a stable base and center point for your stroke.

1 HOW TO CREATE STABILITY
I recommend using Pro Rotating Discs when you practice (*www.optp.com. $79.95*). Set the discs under your feet at address, then try to make your stroke without pivoting to the left or right. The discs give you immediate feedback if and when you lose your stability—you'll literally turn to the left or right of your putt line if you use too much body movement. Another good way to check your stability is to stroke putts while standing on foam rollers that have been cut in half (*www. performbetter.com, $15.90/pair*). Poor stability on these things will have you rocking back and forth in a heartbeat.

2 HOW TO CREATE BALANCE
Putt with your head held against a stationary object, like your living room wall or the Bender Stick (*www. benderstick.com, $99.95*), developed by Top 100 Teacher Mike Bender.

Rotating discs immediately show if you lose stability...

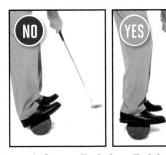

...as do foam roller halves. Training aids that provide immediate feedback are key.

1 STABILITY WORK
Use training aids to force yourself to remain in balance.

NOTES ON FEEDBACK

The best way to practice any fundamental is with feedback, which is why the majority of drills I'll show you over the next several pages involve the use of training aids. Practicing with feedback is critical for improvement. Otherwise you won't know if you're working on the right things or practicing in a way that will groove bad habits.

2 BALANCE WORK
Practice keeping your head still (using a wall or an advanced training aid like this) to help you make your stroke around a central point.

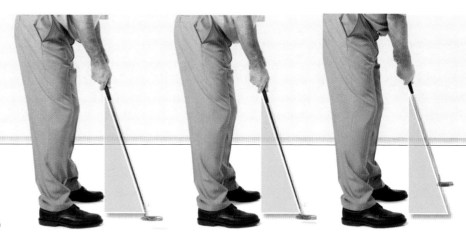

BASIC NO. 2: KEEP YOUR STROKE ON PLANE

The lie of your putter (around 70 degrees) sets the plane of your stroke, and you should maintain this angle from start to finish. To help you with this, imagine that you're making a stroke along the angled roof of a house—gently scrape the shaft along the shingles.

Imagine that the shaft rests on the roof of a house, and glide it along the roof from start to finish.

AN AID THAT WORKS

Eyeline Golf's Dual-Plane Putting System is a great tool to help you train your stroke to remain on plane. They're hard to come by (a Web search might come in handy), but you can create your own device with any two solid objects simulating the rails. Here's how it works.

STEP 1

Discover the feel of an on-plane stroke by riding the inside rail (*photo, bottom left*), then by riding the outside rail (*bottom right*). By using both extremes, you'll immediately discover the proper feel of an on-plane stroke, which is critical for success.

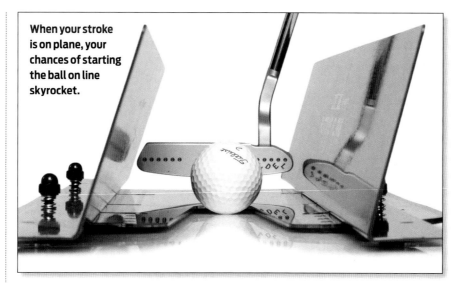

When your stroke is on plane, your chances of starting the ball on line skyrocket.

STEP 2

Once you groove the correct feels in step 1, set up the device for "negative feedback." In other words, your goal now is to execute your stroke without hitting the rails; you get a negative response once you sense that either the toe or heel of your putter touches the rails. Despite the misleading terminology, negative feedback is more powerful than positive feedback when it comes to helping you turn a good feel into a solid habit.

STROKE BASIC NO. 3:
ZERO SHAFT ROTATION

Never, ever allow the puttershaft to twist around its own axis when you putt.

BASIC NO. 3:
DON'T TWIST THE SHAFT

If you want to improve your putting accuracy, eliminate undue putterface manipulation by making a zero-shaft-rotation stroke. In other words, don't twist the shaft as you practice your motion along the imaginary roof as shown on the previous page. Keep in mind that this doesn't have anything to do with the putterface, which certainly rotates *relative to the line of the putt* in a solid stroke. It only applies to the shaft, and **if you keep it from rotating, then the putterface will open in your backstroke and close in your forward-stroke, yet remain square to the arcing path of your stroke at all times.**

If you rotate the shaft as you stroke back and through, you'll produce the excessive putterface rotation shown in the picture above right, generated from a poor stroke captured by SAM PuttLab, the industry's most sophisticated tool for measuring putting strokes. If you do it right, then your stroke will be more like the SAM graphic below right.

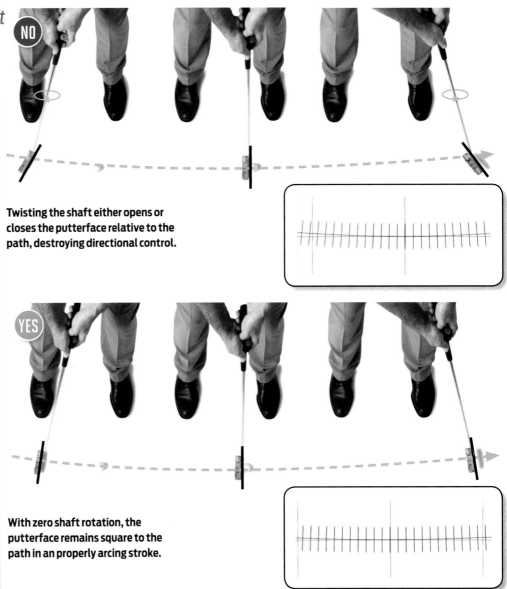

Twisting the shaft either opens or closes the putterface relative to the path, destroying directional control.

With zero shaft rotation, the putterface remains square to the path in an properly arcing stroke.

Video lessons from the greatest putting instructors in the game at **golf.com/putting** *and on the tablet editions of* Golf Magazine

HOW TO PRACTICE A ZERO-SHAFT-ROTATION PUTTING STROKE

Place a mirror to your immediate right along your putting line and make practice putting strokes with a tennis racket to get a feel for a zero-shaft-rotation stroke. **If you "putt" with the tennis racket correctly, then you'll only see the sides of the racket at address, in your backstroke and in your forward-stroke as you check your progress in the mirror.** If you twist, or rotate, the shaft at any point during your motion, you'll see the strings.

Take this drill a step further and set the racket against the bottom of the edge of a tabletop or desk. Here, keep the broad side of the frame in contact with the edge from start to finish. If you rotate the racket, one side of the frame will lose contact with the edge of the table.

This is a great exercise. The flat front of a tennis racket is ideal for exposing any rotation in your putting motion. It's easy to do, and you can practice it at home or in your office. The greater the effort you put into practicing this drill, the more you'll help your directional control on the course.

Only the sides of the tennis racket visible at address...

...and at the end of your backstroke...

...and as you swing the racket through impact. At no point should you ever catch glimpse of the strings.

STROKE BASIC NO. 4:
PUTT WITH A FULCRUM

Motion your putter back and through around a central point.

BASIC NO. 4: PUTT AROUND A CENTRAL POINT

A fulcrum, or central pivot point in your stroke, is another great quality to have in your putting motion. You can anchor your fulcrum against your body with a long or belly putter or employ a virtual fulcrum if you prefer putting with a conventional flatstick. **Basically, your fulcrum represents the center point of your stroke, and you'll make the best contact if you motion your putterhead around this point.**

Check the graphics generated by SAM PuttLab at right. The red lines represent the puttershaft and the blue lines show where the shaft is pointing throughout the stroke. As you may suspect, the clear presence of a tight fulcrum in the far graphic is ideal: the stroke is motioning back and through around a very defined central point, with the shaft pointing at the same spot from beginning to end. The golfer who made this stroke is regarded as one of the top putters on the PGA Tour.

The near graphic, on the other hand, lacks a clearly noticeable fulcrum: the blue lines don't overlap in the same spot like they do in the pro example. The putter isn't motioning back and through around a defined center. Instead, the player is manipulating it from start to finish.

The quality of your fulcrum is a good predictor of your ability to control the ball on the greens. If yours isn't tight and clearly defined, then you're going to struggle.

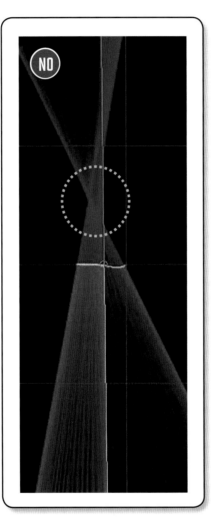

The width of the area where the blue lines cross indicates that this golfer is manipulating his stroke rather than motioning it around a central point. Poor contact and control are the results.

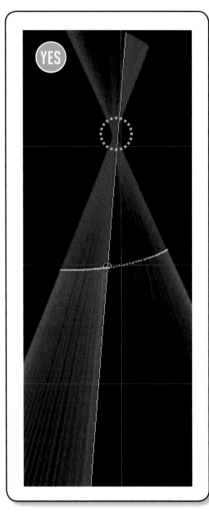

The tight dispersion of the blue lines at the intersection point indicates that this putter—a PGA Tour pro—is motioning the putter correctly, pointing the shaft at the same spot from start to finish.

PHYSICAL FULCRUM
When the fulcrum of your stroke is physically anchored to your body, like it is with a belly or long putter or if you use a pure wrist stroke, you're more apt to pivot your stroke around a central point, giving you enhanced putterhead control. This is one of the reasons for the surge in popularity of belly and long putters.

VIRTUAL FULCRUM
With a conventional putter and most stroke styles, the fulcrum of your motion is merely a point in space, since no part of the putter is in contact with your body. A virtual fulcrum makes for a more challenging stroke, but it's a challenge that has successfully been met by great putters since the invention of the game.

"THE QUALITY OF YOUR FULCRUM IS A GOOD PREDICTOR OF YOUR ABILITY TO CONTROL THE BALL ON THE GREENS."

HOW TO ESTABLISH AND MAINTAIN A
PUTTING FULCRUM

Anchor your stroke for better contact and speed control and putts that always start on their intended line.

STRIVE FOR A UNIFIED STROKE

Losing your fulcrum creates a haphazard motion that will make controlling your putter—and the ball—very challenging. A good way to keep your fulcrum nice and tight is to **keep the "Y" structure formed by your arms and the puttershaft at address intact from start to finish.** This will help unify your stroke so that there are fewer moving parts. The secret, however, is to build the "Y" using six key pressure points.

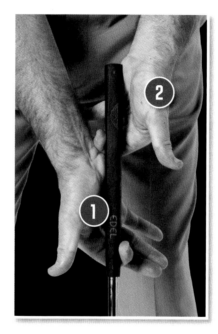

Pressure lost in hands.

Pressure lost on left side.

SIX POINTS OF PRESSURE

When you take your grip and settle into your stance, make sure you feel pressure in the following six areas. (*Check their positions in the photos above and right.*) Pressure here allows you to correctly build the "Y" at address and maintain it—and your fulcrum—throughout your motion.

1. *Heel pad of right palm*
2. *Heel pad of left palm*
3. *Right-hand fingers*
4. *Left-hand fingers*
5. *Right-arm connection to chest*
6. *Left-arm connection to chest*

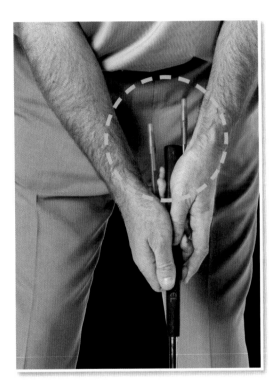

HOW TO MAINTAIN CORRECT PRESSURE IN YOUR HANDS

You should feel like the heel pad on each hand is pushing into the grip while your fingers are pulling it. This push/pull feeling stabilizes your arms, hands and putter, helping you to create and maintain the "Y." To ingrain this feel, place pens or tees in between the heel pad of each hand and the grip. Make some practice strokes and see if you can maintain proper pressure and hold the items in place from start to finish. You don't need a lot of pressure, but you don't want to make the mistake of using too loose a grip either.

HOW TO MAINTAIN CORRECT PRESSURE BETWEEN YOUR ARMS AND CHEST

If you tend to lose the pressure points in your arms (Nos. 5 and 6) place a glove or head cover under each armpit. Your goal is to make your stroke without the glove or head cover dropping to the ground. Just like the third leg of a tripod, pressure between your arms and chest provides structure. Putting without pressure points is also like driving a bike with loose spokes—it may work some of the time, but it sure won't be pretty and you'll never pedal it straight.

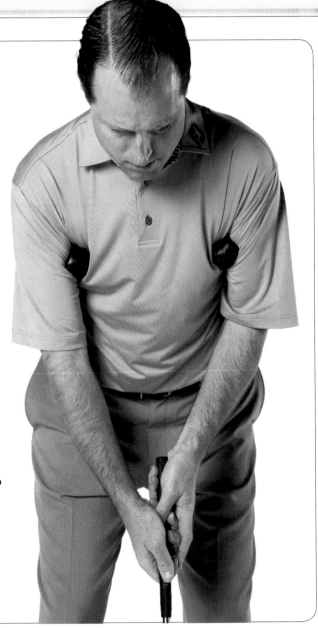

STROKE BASIC NO. 5:
TEMPO

The timing of your stroke has as much influence on how far you hit your putts as stroke length, so you better get it right.

BASIC NO. 5: CONTROL SPEED WITH TEMPO

The amount of time it takes great putters to complete their strokes is consistent from one putt to the next. **A repetitive tempo is critical for speed and distance control.** It doesn't matter if you're hitting a 70-foot lag putt, a sliding 16-footer or a short knee-knocker to halve the hole, your tempo—the time it takes to complete your stroke—never changes. Finding and repeating your tempo allows your "inner athlete" to control distance simply by changing the length of your stroke. If you're constantly changing tempo, then you have too many variables working at the same time to roll the ball the correct distance on a consistent basis.

LONG PUTT
Make a longer stroke, not a faster one.

SHORT PUTT
Make a shorter stroke, not a slower one.

NOTES ON TEMPO

Using consistent tempo allows the athlete within you to sense the speed of your putts. Inconsistent tempo is a sure sign that you're trying to steer the ball. Not only can proper tempo improve the quality of your roll, working on it can also help you improve your self-management skills. If you find yourself caring so much about a putt that your stroke gets tight and doesn't flow, focus even more on your tempo, using it as a physical cue to solve a mental barrier.

Video lessons and drills to instantly improve your putting at golf.com/putting and on the tablet editions of Golf Magazine

Practicing your stroke to the beat of a metronome is the fast way to improve your putting tempo and rhythm.

HOW TO PRACTICE YOUR TEMPO

I recommend working on your tempo by first downloading a metronome app to your smartphone. There are dozens of quality products out there. Run the app and begin experimenting with the ticktock sound set at different speeds. You'll quickly find that anything less than 60 beats per minute (bpm) on the metronome is a little bit on the slow side, and at this tempo you're probably guiding the putter instead of swinging it. If you set the metronome above 90 bpm, you run the risk of practicing a stroke that's more forced than smooth.

As you work with the metronome, look for a speed that's merely comfortable—forget about finding perfection. They key is the consistency of your timing and not the timing itself.

To get in touch with the beat of the metronome, use a four-beat phrase like "one two back through" or, my personal favorite, the three-beat phrase "ready to there." I like this one because you get the timing benefit plus a nice reminder to focus on your target.

"FINDING AND REPEATING YOUR TEMPO ALLOWS YOUR 'INNER ATHLETE' TO CONTROL DISTANCE SIMPLY BY CHANGING THE LENGTH OF YOUR STROKE."

STROKE BASIC NO. 6:
ACCELERATION

How fast is too fast? How slow is too slow? Here's how to nail the speed of your stroke to create the perfect blend of motion and control.

BASIC NO. 6: GET THE RIGHT STROKE SPEED

Just as with tempo, great putters have a consistent acceleration pattern in their strokes, and whatever these acceleration patterns are, they repeat them. **Making a stroke with proper acceleration is like driving a stick shift: you don't want to stall the engine (because you were too careful) nor spin the wheels (because you slammed down on the gas pedal).** Doing it correctly allows you to motion your putter without forcing or steering it into impact.

Try the following to get a feel for what I'm talking about: hold the grip end of your wedge in your left hand with just your thumb and middle finger on the handle and then gently swing it back and forth like a pendulum. This natural swinging motion is based almost exclusively on acceleration and natural forces like gravity and momentum. Next, grab your putter with your right hand and copy the motion of the wedge with your putter. (Continue swinging the wedge with your left hand.) Once you get the feel for the rhythm of each club, slow the putter down. How does it feel now? Can you sense how you've manipulated its acceleration and how

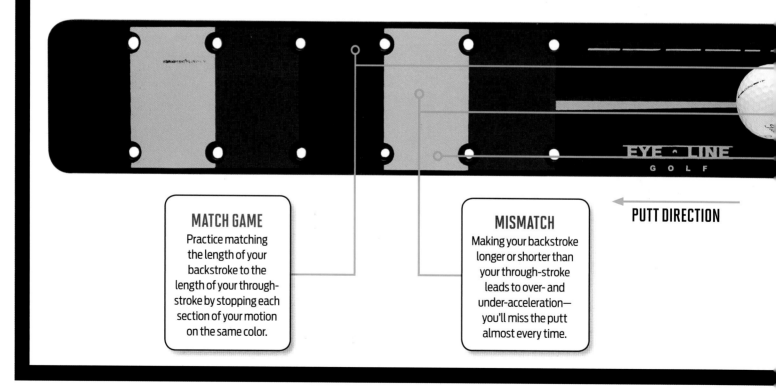

PUTT DIRECTION

MATCH GAME
Practice matching the length of your backstroke to the length of your through-stroke by stopping each section of your motion on the same color.

MISMATCH
Making your backstroke longer or shorter than your through-stroke leads to over- and under-acceleration— you'll miss the putt almost every time.

NOTES ON ACCELERATION

Here's the deal: good putters accelerate up to a certain point, then maintain that acceleration through the ball. Doing so means less manipulation (i.e., a pure stroke). Bad putters, on the other hand, are constantly accelerating, and almost always hit max speed after impact. The best analogy for controlling speed is a car approaching a bridge. If I asked you to reach the bridge going exactly 60 mph, how would you go about doing it? You wouldn't accelerate all the way up to the bridge and hope you time it right so that you hit 60 right when you get to the bridge. Rather, you'd get to 60 mph as fast as you could, then maintain that rate of speed until you reached the bridge.

this could potentially lead to a mis-hit or missed putt? Now go in the other direction and swing your putter faster than your wedge. Can you sense the manipulated thrust needed to motion the putter at a quicker pace? Does it make sense that both speed and directional control would be challenging if you used similar thrust when you putted? Keep swinging your putter at different speeds like this. Once you have a definitive answer for each of the questions, you'll start to get the right idea about acceleration and about how to apply proper speed to your motion.

HOW TO PRACTICE ACCELERATION

The Speed Board (*below*), developed by fellow *GOLF Magazine* Top 100 teacher Todd Sones, is a great tool to help you develop an effective acceleration profile (*www.eyelinegolf. com, $29.95*). To use it, set a ball in the middle of the board as shown and practice making strokes that hit the same color block on both sides of impact (red to red, yellow to yellow, etc.). Perform the drill as a discovery exercise at first with no target in mind—simply learn the feel of a balanced stroke. The benefit of doing this on the Speed Board is that it provides visual cues for you to match the length of your backstroke to that of your through-stroke. This is important for acceleration because strokes that are too short-to-long tend to over-accelerate through impact and strokes that are too long-to-short tend to be sluggish and "steery" through impact.

SAM PuttLab research suggests that, for most golfers, matching stroke lengths on both sides of the ball or making the through-stroke slightly longer allows for solid speed and directional control.

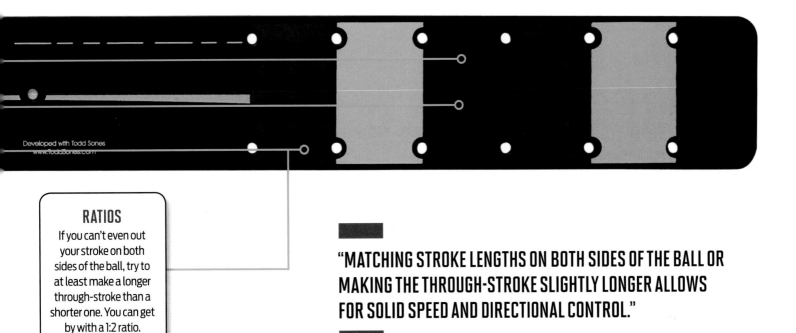

Developed with Todd Sones
www.toddsones.com

RATIOS

If you can't even out your stroke on both sides of the ball, try to at least make a longer through-stroke than a shorter one. You can get by with a 1:2 ratio.

"MATCHING STROKE LENGTHS ON BOTH SIDES OF THE BALL OR MAKING THE THROUGH-STROKE SLIGHTLY LONGER ALLOWS FOR SOLID SPEED AND DIRECTIONAL CONTROL."

STROKE BASIC NO. 7:
USE THE BEST ENGINE

You can motor the putter in any one of four ways. Here's how to find the engine that works best for you and your putter.

TORSO ENGINE

Fulcrum: In line with the shaft on a spot on your chest at about the same height as the logo on your shirt.
How to Do It: Picture the "Y" formed by your arms and your putter at address and try to maintain it all the way into your follow-through.
How to Feel It: Hold your arms across your chest and rotate your upper torso to the left and right while keeping your legs steady.

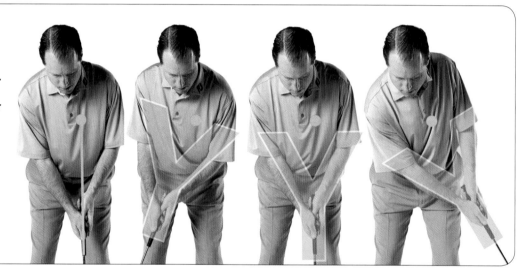

ELBOW ENGINE

Fulcrum: In line with the shaft but set lower on your torso. (Players who successfully putt with a belly putter use this engine at least as a complement to a torso engine, or may use it exclusively.)
How to Do It: Pull your right elbow back and bend it in your backswing and pull your left elbow forward and bend it in your through-stroke.
How to Feel It: Picture a sprinter running at top speed—one elbow pulls back and the other swings forward with each stride.

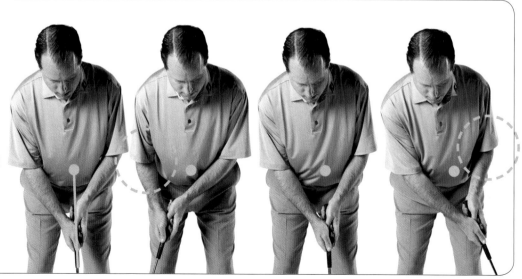

BASIC NO. 7: START YOUR ENGINES!

There are many different ways to motion the putter back and through that allow you to meet the demands of the stroke basics discussed thus far, but these are variations of four primary putting motors: 1) your torso/shoulders, 2) your elbows, 3) your wrists and 4) a wrist-arm piston motion. Although it's perfectly okay to combine different parts of these engines to make your stroke your own, clearly identifying one of them as your primary motor will allow you to execute a solid stroke without having to rely on too many swing thoughts and images. The simpler the better. The fewer moving parts you have to deal with the more focused you can be on what you're really trying to accomplish in your stroke.

WRIST ENGINE

Fulcrum: Either your left wrist or your right wrist, which allows you to putt with a physical fulcrum.

How to Do It: Hinge your wrists back and forward without moving your hands or arms out of the position they hold at address.

How to Feel It: Practice the hinging action while focusing on how the cap of the grip stays in the same place, like the top end of a pendulum.

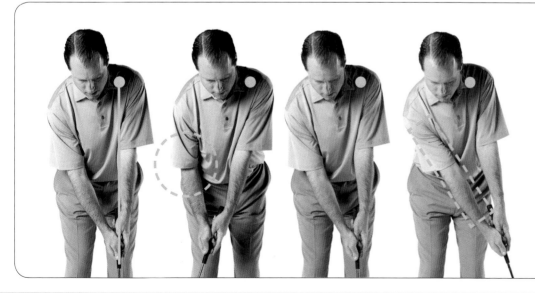

PISTON ENGINE

Fulcrum: Your left shoulder or the spot where you anchor a long putter if that's what you use. (Having a physical fulcrum, as you do with a long putter works best with this style.)

How to Do It: Pull your right elbow back and bend it in your backstroke, then push it forward while straightening your elbow in your follow-through.

How to Feel It: Practice the right-elbow motion above while keeping your upper body very still.

HOW TO
SET UP FOR SUCCESS

Standing to the ball correctly and with the proper posture is the easiest way to make sure you hit the key stroke fundamentals.

It may seem backward to begin talking about your setup so late in this chapter. The reason why I've waited until now is that **it's impossible for you to make informed decisions about your setup without first knowing what you're trying to accomplish in your stroke,** but now that

you understand the key stroke concepts, you can think about your setup in way that allows you to exploit and master them.

HOW TO DO IT
The clap exercise can help you build the correct stance time and again.

STEP 1
Get into a strong and balanced position with your arms hanging straight down in front of you. Set your feet shoulder width apart and bend your upper body toward the ball.

STEP 2
Without moving anything else, clap your hands together. This automatically aligns your forearms—if you were to look at a mirror on your right you'd only see your right forearm.

STEP 3
Pull your elbows in toward your sides so that your upper arms are comfortably connected to your body. This is key to promoting a zero-shaft-rotation stroke.

STEP 4
Point your index fingers at the ball. As you do this, check that your eyes are over the inside edge of the ball. This is important since eye position seriously influences aim.

STEP 5
Set the putterhead behind the ball. If your putter is the right fit for you, the shaft will line up with your forearms, placing you in perfect position to make an on-plane stroke.

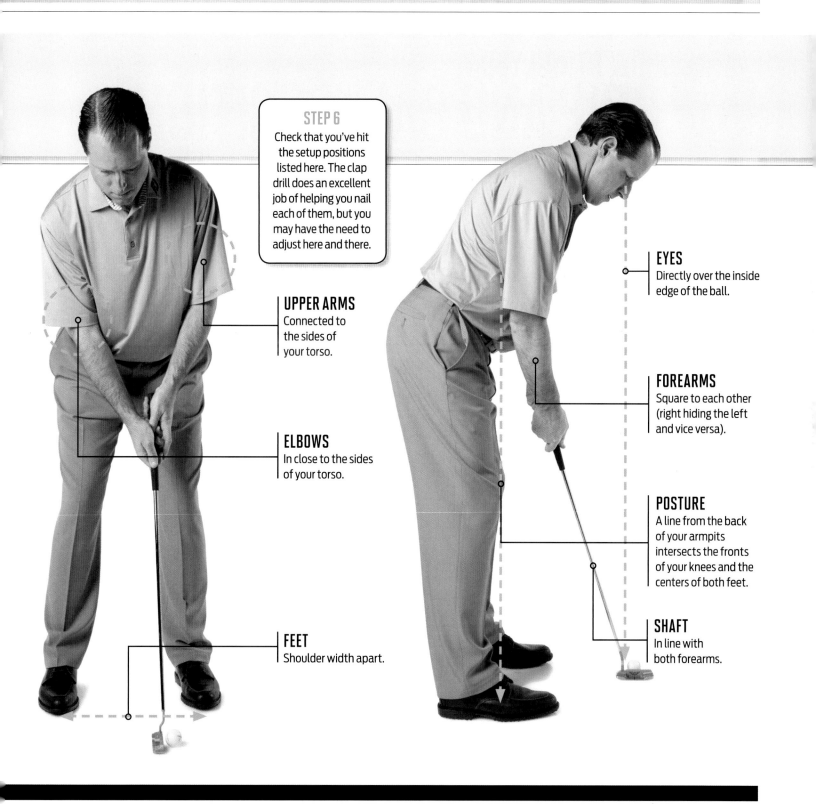

STEP 6

Check that you've hit the setup positions listed here. The clap drill does an excellent job of helping you nail each of them, but you may have the need to adjust here and there.

UPPER ARMS
Connected to the sides of your torso.

ELBOWS
In close to the sides of your torso.

FEET
Shoulder width apart.

EYES
Directly over the inside edge of the ball.

FOREARMS
Square to each other (right hiding the left and vice versa).

POSTURE
A line from the back of your armpits intersects the fronts of your knees and the centers of both feet.

SHAFT
In line with both forearms.

HOW TO NAIL YOUR
GRIP AND BALL POSITION

Here's where you can add to the individuality of your stroke. When it comes to ball position and grip, it's all about what feels best to you.

CHOOSE YOUR GRIP

Try one or try them all. One will feel best to you and allow you to nail each of the basics covered in this chapter better than the rest.

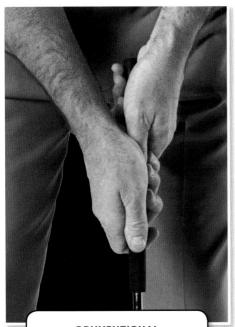

CONVENTIONAL
The basic putting hold features hands that square to each other as well as to your body lines—neither one is supinated (rotated palm up) or pronated (rotated palm down). This creates a neutral arm position that's ideal for promoting an on-plane, zero-shaft-rotation stroke.

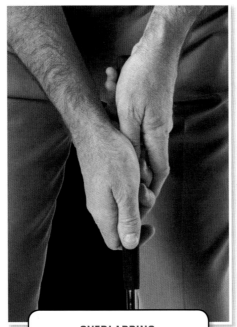

OVERLAPPING
Same as the conventional grip, with the only difference being that the left index finger overlaps the fingers of the right hand instead of wrapping around the handle. This is just one of countless ways to bring your hands together. The key is to find one that feels good and allows you to set your forearms square.

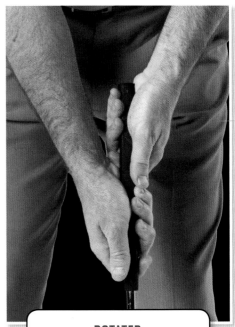

ROTATED
This is a copy of a style used by the late Paul Runyan, a two-time PGA Championship winner in the 1930s who went on to become one of the game's finest teachers. Turning both hands 45 degrees under the grip like Runyan did makes it easier to secure pressure points 1–4 (*page 150*) and establish a fulcrum.

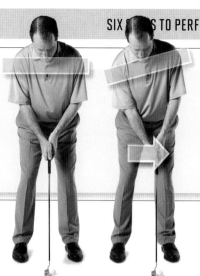

SELECT YOUR BALL POSITION

As long as you adhere to the setup-position basics outlined on pages 158 and 159, position the ball in your stance wherever it feels the most comfortable. There are no rules for ball position, but keep in mind that the farther you play the ball up in your stance (*photo, far right*), the more your right shoulder needs to dip below your left, and the more you need to move your hands forward.

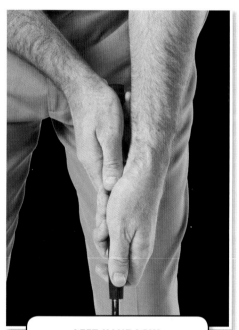

LEFT-HAND LOW

Gripping the handle with the left hand below the right causes the left arm to extend fully at address. This provides two technical advantages: 1) it eliminates unwanted right-wrist action and 2) it sets the left wrist flat while bending the right. This flat/bent combination ensures correct pressure and, as a result, a proper fulcrum.

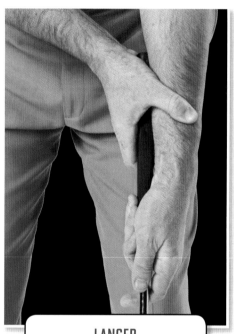

LANGER

Bernhard Langer created this adaptation of the left-hand-low grip to successfully cure his yips. As is the case with the rotated grip, this style allows the player who uses it to effectively engage pressure points 1—4 (*page 150*).

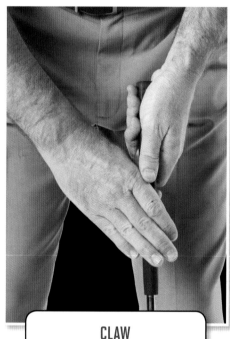

CLAW

This grip has helped countless number of players who inadvertently use their right wrist as an engine. Rotating the right palm so that the right wrist runs parallel to the direction of the stroke takes this troublesome joint completely out of the picture.

HOW TO
ALIGN TO YOUR TARGET

*Great putters align their bodies very differently.
Here's how to find the method that's right for you.*

ALIGNMENT OPTIONS

Some players prefer to set everything—feet, hips, chest, forearms, shoulders, eyes and putterface—parallel to their target line (*photo, below left*). Others get aligned by setting their bodies more open to the target line (aimed left) if only because they feel that they see putts better this way (*below center*). The choice is yours. A word of caution, however: if you play from an open stance (à la Jack Nicklaus), make sure that it's just your stance that's open and not your whole body. There's nothing wrong with opening up your feet—or even your hips—when you set up, but when it comes to your shoulders and forearms, it's critical that you set them square to the line. Notice in the picture below right how opening my body—even from a square stance—moves my forearms out of alignment. You can clearly see both forearms (but you can only see my left forearm in the photos below center and right). This is important because your forearms must be square for you to execute an on-plane stroke.

CATCH A TRAIN
The image of a railroad track running through your line can help you set the putterface square to your target. Align your feet parallel left of the track or open to the line, depending on your preference.

YES   **YES**   **NO**

Body and stance square.   Body square, stance open.   Body open.

Video lessons from the greatest putting instructors in the game at **golf.com/putting** *and on the tablet editions of* Golf Magazine

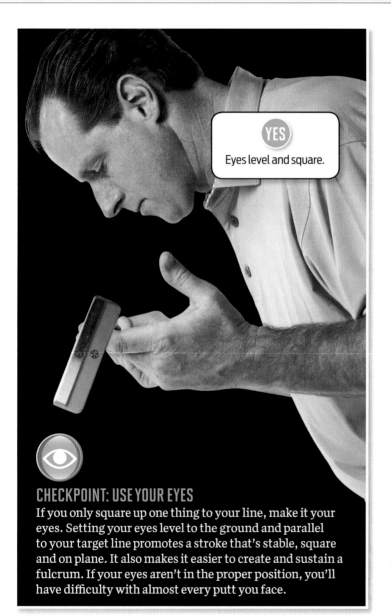

YES
Eyes level and square.

CHECKPOINT: USE YOUR EYES

If you only square up one thing to your line, make it your eyes. Setting your eyes level to the ground and parallel to your target line promotes a stroke that's stable, square and on plane. It also makes it easier to create and sustain a fulcrum. If your eyes aren't in the proper position, you'll have difficulty with almost every putt you face.

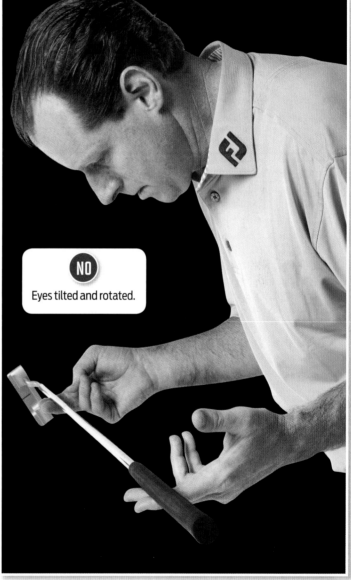

NO
Eyes tilted and rotated.

HOW TO BECOME A
CONSISTENT PUTTER

My setup-reminder drill gets you in all of the right positions every time you putt—just like the pros do.

LEARN FROM THE PROS

Have you ever wondered why the best putters are so good at what they do and, more importantly, how they got there? A lot have golfers have, and unfortunately there hasn't been a suitable answer, but I think I know their secret. **Great putters are great if only because they are *consistent*, and they reach elite status by being *purposeful* in everything they do.** They practice their technique and approach every putt with a carefully devised plan, and in executing this plan they leave nothing to chance, even with something as simple as stance width or how far they stand from the ball at address. Do minute elements of your setup such as these really matter? A student of mine recently came up with the best answer I've ever heard to this question: "In golf, millimeters matter."

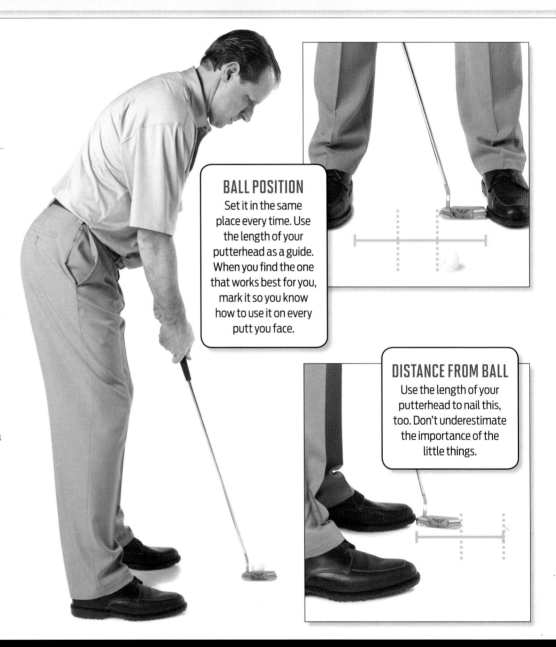

BALL POSITION
Set it in the same place every time. Use the length of your putterhead as a guide. When you find the one that works best for you, mark it so you know how to use it on every putt you face.

DISTANCE FROM BALL
Use the length of your putterhead to nail this, too. Don't underestimate the importance of the little things.

"IN GOLF, MILLIMETERS MATTER."

MAKE A PUTTING FOOTPRINT

If you want consistent outcomes, you need to put forth consistent performance, which will require that you pay attention to details. As soon as you finish this chapter, visit **golf.com/basicsbook** to download special putting footprint and putting setup matrix forms to help you make key decisions about your address position and overall technique.

The footprint form tells you how to construct an address-position practice station like the one pictured here. All you'll have to do is take your best stance and have a friend draw lines around your feet and the ball. **This gives you a ground-level reference for the stance width, ball position and distance from the ball that allow you to putt your best.** Plus, whenever your putts start to miss or you begin to feel that your stroke isn't working correctly, you can step into your footprint and regain all the right feels.

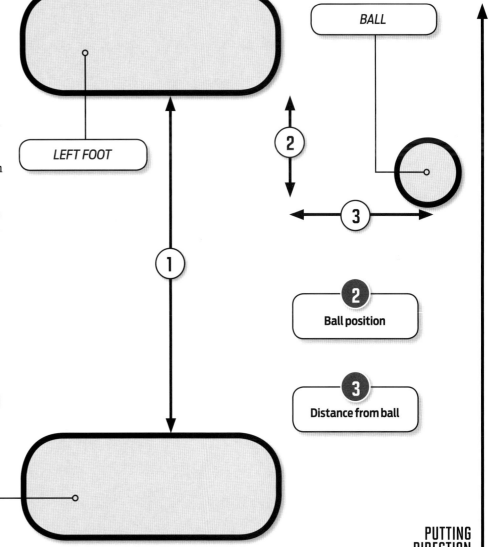

BALL

LEFT FOOT

2

3

RIGHT FOOT

1 Stance width

2 Ball position

3 Distance from ball

PUTTING DIRECTION

HOW TO
PRACTICE LIKE A PRO

Use your practice or warm-up time wisely to add accuracy, distance control and high-level performance to your stroke.

Y ou have no problem spending four hours to complete a round, an extra hour having drinks in the clubhouse and the time it takes to get to and from the course. Yet you can't spend 15 to 30 minutes before your round to properly warm up your process and stroke. Even when you do, you go about it in the wrong way, blindly rolling balls on the practice green with zero motivation toward building something positive in your technique.

If you're okay with spending six hours or more to get in a round of golf, then you should be okay with arriving at the course just 20 minutes earlier and getting into the right putting mindset using the drills on the opposite page, which are designed to get you accustomed to sinking putts. Most amateurs practice the act of missing, choosing to hit putts *toward* a hole. Good practice means doing things that get the ball *in* the hole. Try the drills and see if they don't get your stroke motoring out of the blocks on the key opening holes. On your days away from the course, use them at the range to keep your technique razor sharp between rounds.

"MOST AMATEURS PRACTICE THE ACT OF MISSING, CHOOSING TO HIT PUTTS *TOWARD* A HOLE."

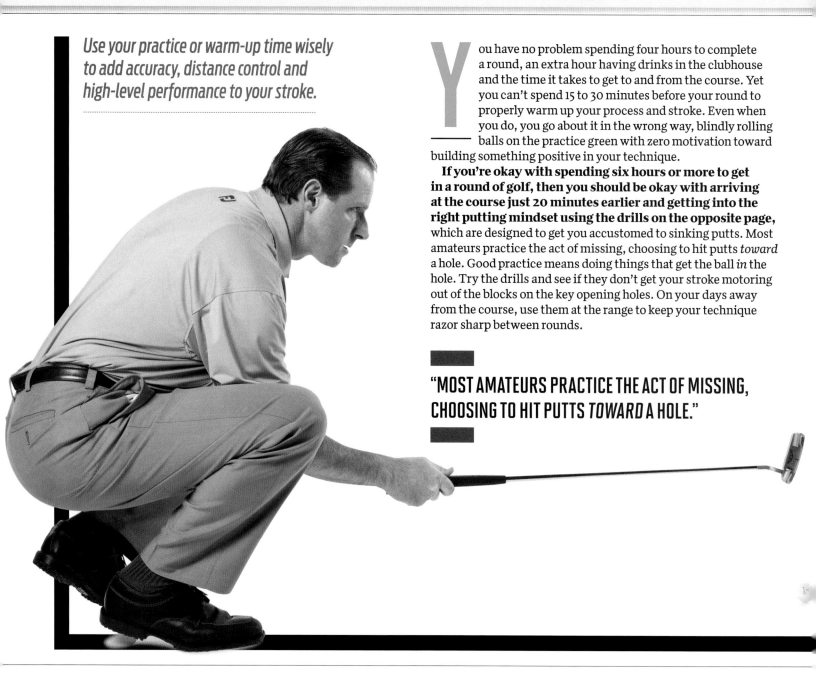

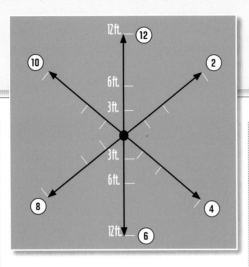

DRILL 1: STRAIGHT UP THE HILL

What It Does: Increases directional control.

How to Do It: Begin two feet from a hole on a flat section of the practice green and start putting a few 2-footers. At this point, focus on steps 3–5 of the putting process: feel it, get set and go!

On each attempt from this distance, notice what it takes to roll the ball in the middle of the hole. Do you need better forearm alignment? Or maybe you need to focus on staying centered and stable. Whatever it is, make sure you're controlling direction (i.e., rolling the ball straight) on each putt.

After you make a few from 2 feet, hit some putts from 3 feet. After draining a few from there, move back to 5 feet and then 10 feet. Don't move to a new distance until you feel that you're nailing steps 3-5 and using this part of the putting process to control the direction of each attempt.

Depending on how much time you have, try to perform the drill from 15 feet before moving on to the exercise at right. You'll need about five minutes to complete it—a little time for a lot of extra accuracy.

DRILL 2: PUTT AROUND THE CLOCK

What It Does: Helps you improve your ability in each step of the putting process.

How to Do It: Now that you have some directional control, work on your ability to adjust for variances in distance and slope by rolling balls from all 12 "hours" around the cup, preferably on a sloping section of the green so that you can experience right and left breaks as well as uphill and downhill putts. If time doesn't allow you to completely circle the clock, putt from at least six different angles (*illustration, above*). Practicing like this requires you to start each putt as if you were seeing it for the first time, which is great preparation for what you'll encounter on the course.

As you perform this drill it's important that you go through each step of the putting process in order. Do it correctly and you'll set yourself apart from the other members of your foursome by getting yourself ready to actually make putts instead of just rolling them toward the hole. The difference will be huge.

Hit putts from 3, 6 and 12 feet before moving on to the next station. It should take you about 10 minutes.

DRILL 3: ONE-BALL RANDOM PUTTING

What It Does: Increases speed control.

How to Do It: At this point you're actually pretty warmed up. You've practiced speed control by sinking uphill putts from different distances (drill 1) and a few nasty breaking putts (drill 2). What you need to do now is repeat these skills and make putts *on your first attempt*.

For this last drill, simply pick a hole on the practice putting green (it doesn't matter how far away it is), putt to it and, whether you sink the putt or not, immediately take aim at another hole. The idea is to challenge your ability to successfully read putts with respect to direction and speed on your first try. Practicing this way (do it for 10 minutes) is critical since you don't get a second chance when you're out on the course.

As you perform this drill, really mix it up. Follow an uphill 20-footer with a 40-footer that runs downhill. Then, a nasty 10-foot slider. Important: move on after each putt. You have already practiced your ability to make the short ones, so stick to mastering this final task.

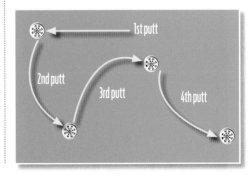

MODIFYING YOUR SWING TO HIT THE SHOTS YOU NEED

How to adapt your basic full and short swings—and keep them from breaking down during your rounds—to meet the demands of an ever-changing game

YOUR GUIDE TO
SHOT SHAPING & SHOT FIXING

INSIDE
Three ways to learn
the basics you need:

LESSONS
Tips and instruction
to help you master
fundamental moves
and positions

CHECKPOINTS
Tests to see if you're
keeping up or falling
behind in your quest to
build a better game

DRILLS
Practice tips and
step-by-step exercises
to make new moves
second nature

Go from beginner to cagey veteran by tweaking your basic swing motion to shape the ball and execute the key shots every player needs.

By now you should be intimately familiar with the basic techniques for setting up consistently, making a fundamentally solid full swing, adjusting your motion for longer clubs, getting up and down from around the green and sinking putts with regularity. You're in a good spot. **But when you're out on the course you'll find that these basic strategies don't always apply.** The course is a varied landscape—you can't expect a perfect lie on every shot you face. Then there are external factors like the weather that demand a little more from your motion. And you're bound to miss shots here and there, placing you in situations where ordinary swing basics have little chance of getting the job done.

Enter shotmaking: the creative ability to adjust for the randomness of the game by curving, bending, lofting, punching and rolling the ball from every lie imaginable. Normally this skill is reserved for seasoned players with experience—and the benefit of trial and error—on their side. In the pages of this chapter, however, I'll bring you right up to their speed, even if you're just starting out or have never attempted a shotmaking play in your life.

The secret, like much of the instruction in this book, is simplicity. I'm going to show you how to hit 11 shots you'll probably have a use for every time you play by simply modifying the moves you've already learned in the previous chapters—tweaks to your setup, backswing, downswing and impact position that allow you to control trajectory and distance and put the ball exactly where it needs to go. And to make sure you don't end up in places that require a specialty shot, I've added a series of on-course fixes to stop 10 common swing faults—and stop them immediately in their tracks. Armed with this information you'll know how to get out of dicey situations as well as avoid getting into them in the first place.

"THE COURSE IS A
VARIED LANDSCAPE—
YOU CAN'T EXPECT A
PERFECT LIE ON
EVERY SHOT
YOU FACE."

YOUR SHOT SHAPING ADVISER

GOLF MAGAZINE
TOP 100 TEACHERS IN AMERICA

KELLIE STENZEL
Palm Beach Golf Course and
Palm Beach Country Club, Palm Beach, Fla.
Golf Magazine Top 100 Teacher (2009–present)
● LPGA and PGA member
● Author, *Women's Guide to Consistent Golf*
● Top 50 Women Teachers in America
● Teaching since 1990
www.kelliestenzelgolf.com

PART 1:
BASIC SHOTMAKING

How to hit 11 score-saving shots in situations where run-of-the-mill swing techniques just won't do.

Good players don't allow tough situations to affect their scores. In fact, they look forward to turning the tables on difficult lies. **You know you have this scorer's attitude the moment you start seeing defensive situations as opportunities to do something special.** You get it by developing a well-rounded game, or put another way, one that allows you to manage your way around the course without having to rely on a single shot shape. This means arming your game with a reliable set of specialty swings. You don't need an arsenal of plays, but rather a few basic swings capable of handling the majority of on-course predicaments. In part 1 of this chapter I'll show you how to execute the 11 most important.

SHOT 1:
THE KNOCKDOWN

WHAT IT IS

A controlled, low-flying shot that travels straight at your target. You hit it with a less-than-full swing, and it's a great play when you're hitting into the wind (keeping the ball low ensures that it won't balloon up into the air and come up short), or if you have to fly the ball under a tree. The knockdown (some people call it a "punch") works with any of your clubs and can help you out on days when your full swing isn't working that well. In fact, it's a solid option even on your good days because the shorter swing used for a knockdown eliminates common errors like overswinging and reverse-pivoting.

HOW TO DO IT

Take one to two extra clubs (a 6- or 7-iron if you're at your 8-iron distance) and follow the steps at right. The ball won't spin much, but you can still play the full distance to your target because this shot tends to sit down almost immediately after it hits.

KNOCKDOWN SETUP ADJUSTMENTS

1. HAND POSITION

Set your hands even with your left thigh so the shaft leans toward the target. This takes loft off the clubface for a lower trajectory.

2. FOOT POSITION

Set the majority of your weight over your left foot and drop the foot back a few inches. Weight here ensures that you make a steeper, more descending swing.

3. BALL POSITION

Play the ball back in your stance, just right of center. This also helps keep the ball low.

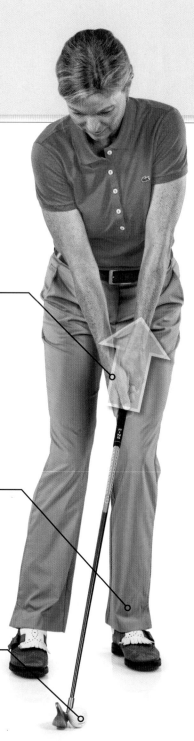

4. THE GRIP

Grip lower on the handle. This gives you extra control.

5. ALIGNMENT

Playing the ball back in your stance typically causes your shoulders to close a little, pointing your body to the right of your target (*photo, below left*). Dropping your left foot back at address re-aligns your shoulders and sets them square to your target line (*below right*), and makes it easy to set your weight over your left side.

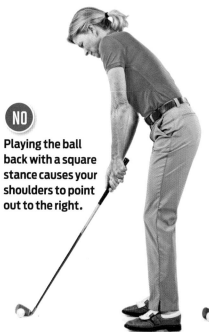

NO Playing the ball back with a square stance causes your shoulders to point out to the right.

YES Drop your left foot back to re-align your shoulders to the target line.

SHOT 1:
THE KNOCKDOWN

Get it close by keeping it low.

The setup positions on the previous pages set the stage for the proper swing motion to hit a knockdown. Keep in mind that **since you set your weight over your left foot at address and the goal is to keep it there when you swing, your backswing automatically will be much shorter.** This is a less-than-full-swing shot—you shouldn't take the club beyond the point when your left arm reaches parallel to the ground (but make sure you fold your right elbow and hinge your left wrist like you learned to do in chapter 2).

KNOCKDOWN BACKSWING
Your backswing is complete when your left arm is parallel to the ground. Actually, your swing should naturally stop at this point because you have most of your weight on your left foot.

NOTES ON TRAJECTORY
Some players use the knockdown when they're hitting with the wind or playing in a crosswind so that the breeze doesn't carry the ball too far.

"IT WON'T MEAN A THING IF YOU CONFUSE 'SHORT' WITH 'SOFT.'"

KNOCKDOWN FOLLOW-THROUGH

Just like you did in your backswing, abbreviate your finish, but make sure that your head, chest, hips and knees are facing the target (like they do in your everyday full swing). The ball will come out low and hot, rising a little but settling quickly once it hits the turf.

KEY MOVE: SWING STRONG

The shaft lean you establish at address helps produce a shorter forward-swing, which is one of the main reasons the ball comes off lower. However, it won't mean a thing if you confuse "short" with "soft." Make an aggressive move from the top, keeping your left hand firm and using your body turn to move your left arm from its horizontal position in your backswing to a vertical position at impact. **As you power through the ball, keep your arms moving forward so that the clubhead doesn't pass your hands (a move that adds loft to the clubface).** The last thing you want on this shot is extra loft. You did it right if the length of your backswing is the same as your forward-swing.

DIFFICULTY LEVEL

● ● ● ◐ ○

Anytime you have to control swing length, it becomes easy to lose your natural rhythm and tempo. On the range, practice keeping the same speed both back and through.

SHOT RECIPE

Club:	One to two more than the distance
Aim:	At target
Stance:	Left foot pulled back
Ball:	Positioned right of center
Swing:	Compact both back and through
Feel:	Keep your left hand firm

SHOT 2:
THE BUMP-AND-RUN

This classic short-game shot gets the ball rolling on the ground quickly so you can better control distance.

WHAT IT IS

A slightly bigger version of your basic chip swing that's designed to travel a few yards in the air (the bump) and then scamper along the ground to your target (the run). Consider using it when you have more room to roll the ball (either on a smooth section of fairway or the green itself) than you do to carry it and there's nothing blocking your route to the pin. **This is a great shot for less-experienced golfers because a shot that travels mostly on the ground is easier to control than one that spends most of its time in the air.**

HOW TO DO IT

Use the chip setup and swing motions you developed on pages 102–109 in chapter 4, but with the following adjustments. The key is to swing a little less than hip-high to hip-high in a half-circle shape (*photos, right*), like you're making a giant putting stroke that smoothly brushes the grass through impact.

DIALING IN BUMP-AND-RUN DISTANCES

The technique is easy. The hard part is making sure the ball carries and rolls the correct amounts so you get it close to the hole. Instead of tinkering with your swing, keep the same hip-high motion and change clubs using the guide at right.

Weight forward.

Hip-high backswing.

GAP WEDGE	PITCHING WEDGE	9-IRON
TOTAL DISTANCE:	*TOTAL DISTANCE:*	*TOTAL DISTANCE:*
10 yards	15 yards	25 yards

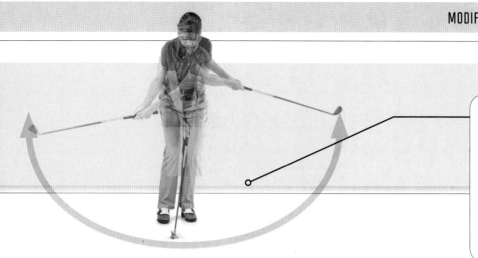

KEY MOVE: STROKE IT LIKE A LONG PUTT

The bump-and-run swing is like a large putting stroke. Set your hands lower on the handle for better accuracy and take a narrow stance (heels three to five inches apart). Set your weight over your left foot at address and keep it there during your swing. This will help you brush the grass under and in front of the ball and create crisp contact, even on tight lies.

Hands leading clubhead.

Brush the grass.

NOTES ON RATIOS

The carry-to-roll ratios you normally use when you chip don't apply to the bump-and-run because more often than not you'll be landing the ball short of the putting surface. That's why you should pull the club based on the total distance you need from the ball to the target.

DIFFICULTY LEVEL

● ○ ○ ○ ○

Two reasons why this shot has been around for hundreds of years: it's easy and it works.

8-IRON
TOTAL DISTANCE:
35 yards

7-IRON
TOTAL DISTANCE:
45 yards

6-IRON
TOTAL DISTANCE:
55 yards

SHOT RECIPE

Club:	*Various*
Aim:	*At target*
Stance:	*Square to slightly open, weight forward*
Ball:	*Positioned slightly right of center*
Swing:	*Hip-high back to hip-high finish*
Feel:	*You're stroking a long putt*

SHOTS 3 & 4:
BALL ABOVE/BELOW FEET

Maintaining your balance and creating solid contact are more important here than anywhere else on the course.

The game would be much easier if you hit every shot from a level lie. But all golfers miss and often find their ball resting on an uneven section of grass. Owning the ability to adjust when the ball is above or below your feet is critical for keeping your scores in the red and making sure you don't follow a bad shot with another. **Your goal on any uneven lie is to achieve solid contact while swinging in balance.** If this means laying up with a shorter club instead of going for the green, then so be it. Lower-handicap golfers may opt for the aggressive play, but my advice to most players is to take a more conservative approach and favor contact and position over distance.

WHAT TO DO WHEN THE BALL IS ABOVE YOUR FEET

ADDRESS
Set your hands lower on the handle to adjust for the fact that the ball is sitting closer to you. Adjust your aim to the right since this lie tends to curve the ball to the left (more so with your longer clubs).

BACKSWING
No need to do anything fancy here. Use your basics from chapter 2. The key is to remain in your address posture. If you feel like the club is swinging back on a flatter plane, don't be concerned. That's just the effect of the slope.

WHAT TO DO WHEN THE BALL IS BELOW YOUR FEET

ADDRESS
Because the ball is farther away from you when it sits below your feet, stand closer to it and hold the club at the very end of the handle. You need every inch of shaft length to get down to the ball.

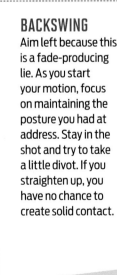

BACKSWING
Aim left because this is a fade-producing lie. As you start your motion, focus on maintaining the posture you had at address. Stay in the shot and try to take a little divot. If you straighten up, you have no chance to create solid contact.

DOWNSWING

The faster you swing, the more likely it is you'll rise up out of your posture and lose your balance. Go at this one at about 80 percent speed and adjust your club selection accordingly.

END SWING

Staying in your address posture is key. So is making a full turn through the ball. You want to finish with your body facing the target, your weight on your front foot and your right foot balanced on its toe.

DIFFICULTY LEVEL

● ● ○ ○ ○

The ball-above-your-feet lie is the easiest of all uneven lies. Just keep leaning into the hill.

SHOT RECIPE

Club:	One to two extra clubs (based on slope)
Aim:	5 to 15 yards right of target
Stance:	Standard
Ball:	Standard position
Swing:	80-percent speed
Feel:	Like you're swinging a baseball bat

DOWNSWING

Take an extra club and swing at 70 percent to help maintain your balance. Plus, they don't call it a longer iron for nothing. That extra half-inch on the next longest club will make it just that much easier to get all the way down to the ball.

END SWING

Since you're fighting gravity the whole way, your turn is more important than ever. Rotating your body to the left from the top acts as a ballast. Strive for a full finish. You should feel like your right shoulder is closer to the target than your left when you end your swing.

DIFFICULTY LEVEL

● ● ● ○ ○

Most people practice only on level lies, so it can be difficult to maintain your balance. This one is easy to catch thin.

SHOT RECIPE

Club:	One extra club
Aim:	5 to 15 yards left of target
Stance:	Just wider than shoulder width
Ball:	Standard position
Swing:	70-percent speed
Feel:	Stay in your address posture

SHOTS 5 & 6:
UPHILL/DOWNHILL LIES

Here are the keys for adjusting your stance and swing when the course has you pointed up and down hills.

A downhill lie typically moves the bottom of your swing arc (where you want to make contact and position the ball in your stance) back, while an uphill lie moves it forward. So if you don't make the right adjustments you're going to hit the ball fat or thin. **On any sloping lie, take a serious practice swing or two and note where the club contacts the ground** (make sure that the slope you take these practice swings on matches the one on which your ball is resting). That point, relative to your stance, is where you need to position the ball when you hit the shot for real. Other than slightly adjusting your weight (*see right*), this is your main concern when you're hitting off a downhill or uphill lie.

WHAT TO DO ON AN UPHILL LIE

ADDRESS
Tilt your body away from the target so that your shoulders, hips and knees match the slope you're standing on. If your shoulders are tilted correctly, your knees will be bent equally and not one more than the other.

BACKSWING
The hill adds loft. Correctly swinging up the slope does, too, turning your 5-iron into a 7-iron. Regardless of the distance to the green, use one to two clubs more than what you normally use for that yardage.

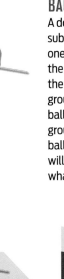

WHAT TO DO ON A DOWNHILL LIE

ADDRESS
Like you do with an uphill lie, match your body to the slope. You can think about this two ways: 1) set your shoulders parallel to the slope or 2) set your spine perpendicular to the slope.

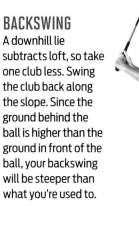

BACKSWING
A downhill lie subtracts loft, so take one club less. Swing the club back along the slope. Since the ground behind the ball is higher than the ground in front of the ball, your backswing will be steeper than what you're used to.

Video lessons on how to handle difficult lies at **golf.com/trouble** *and on the tablet editions of* Golf Magazine

DOWNSWING

Make a three-quarter backswing, then swing down mostly using your arms—you won't be able to shift your weight forward because gravity is pulling you back down the slope. Keep matching your shoulders to the hill.

END SWING

A balanced finish with your weight on your forward foot is important. If you can get to a balanced finish, then you know you won the war against gravity and hit all the way through the shot.

DIFFICULTY LEVEL

● ● ○ ○ ○

If you swing the right club and don't try to do too much with it, your chances of hitting the green are very good.

SHOT RECIPE

Club:	One to two clubs more than the yardage
Aim:	At target
Stance:	Extra wide
Ball:	Standard position
Swing:	Three-quarter backswing and finish
Feel:	Get to a balanced finish on your front foot

DOWNSWING

The proper shoulder tilt allows the club to swing down the hill. You need a sharp downswing to get down to the ball from this lie, but don't forget to turn your hips.

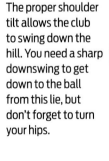
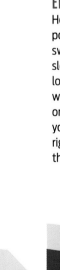

END SWING

Hold a balanced finish position. Since you're swinging down the slope, you'll make a lower follow-through with all of your weight on your left foot. If you hang back on your right side, you'll catch the ball thin or fat.

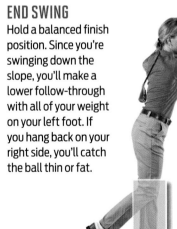

DIFFICULTY LEVEL

● ● ● ◑ ○

If you have trouble properly hitting down on the ball from level lies (or you rarely take divots), you'll hit a low line drive more often than catching it pure.

SHOT RECIPE

Club:	One less than the distance
Aim:	At target
Stance:	Shoulders tilted with the slope
Ball:	Positioned slightly back of center
Swing:	Full back to a low finish
Feel:	You're swinging along the slope

SHOT 7: THE MEGA-LOB

It's high. It's soft. It's exactly what you need to save par from a tough greenside situation.

There will be times when you need more loft than what you get from a basic lob (*pages 118–123*). Most often it'll be when you have to carry an obstacle and stop the ball quickly on the green—a lot of height and not much distance. **The higher you need to fly the ball, the longer your swing needs to be, which is why this is considered a dangerous play.** Pull it off, however, and it's well worth the risk. Beginners should use it sparingly, while those with more experience—or who learn to nail the keys on this page and the next—can use it to turn a tough situation into a memorable par save.

WHAT IT IS

A short lob shot that carries as high in the air as it does over the ground.

DIFFICULTY LEVEL

Success with the mega-lob shot—or any high pitch shot—is driven by feel and experience. Practice will ultimately pay off.

SHOT RECIPE

Club:	*Lob wedge*
Aim:	*Shade left of target*
Stance:	*Slightly open*
Ball:	*Positioned slightly forward of center*
Swing:	*Three-quarters to full*
Feel:	*Bottom of club thumps the ground*

HOW TO PLAY THE MEGA-LOB

1 CLUB SELECTION
Grab your lob wedge or most lofted club. (If you don't carry a lob wedge, you're putting yourself at a disadvantage.) Check that the loft it generates from a square setup is enough for the shot by stepping on the face of the club—the shaft will lift up and give you an idea of how high the ball will launch.

2 SETUP
Position the ball forward in your stance, off your left heel. Playing the ball up gives you extra loft. (Notice how the clubshaft is leaning away from the target.) Weaken your grip until the "V's" formed by your index fingers and thumbs point up the left side of the handle. As you settle into your stance, point the grip at your belly button. This will increase the loft and the bounce of your wedge as well as open your shoulders. You should aim the clubface a yard or two left of the target.

3 BACKSWING

Adjust the length of your backswing, depending on how far you need to fly the ball, but keep in mind that this is a control shot and you really don't need more than a three-quarter backswing. This more compact motion will help you achieve the easy tempo and transition you want for this shot. Swing along your shoulder line (out and across your target line), which will produce a higher and softer-landing shot.

4 DOWNSWING

Make an aggressive downswing and don't stop until you've reached a full finish, with your weight over your front foot. Moving your weight forward like this keeps the clubhead low to the ground after impact. Your goal should be to thump the ground with the underside of your wedge.

SHOT 8:
THE PURPOSEFUL FADE

It's not a slice. It's a secret weapon that's actually pretty easy to pull off.

Y ou're on the tee on a dogleg-right (the hole bends to the right) or with trouble lining the left side of the fairway. Or you're in the fairway, but there are trees on the right that you need to curve the ball around in order to hit the green. Or it could be that you're attacking a front-right pin position. **In any of theses situations, your play is a fade, a shot that curves softly from left to right.**

DIFFICULTY LEVEL

You likely already have an outside-in swing, so all you need to do is swing outside-in a little faster.

SHOT RECIPE

Club:	*Any*
Aim:	*Shoulders open, clubface at target*
Stance:	*Open*
Ball:	*Positioned between center and left heel*
Swing:	*Full speed*
Feel:	*You're holding the clubface open*

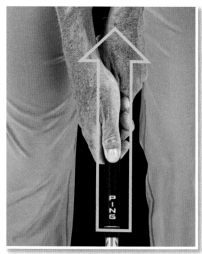

THE FADE GRIP

Use a slightly weaker hold (hands rotated more to the left). This will help produce a more open clubface at impact and a fading ball flight.

Clubshaft pointing straight up and down in your finish.

THE FADE SETUP
Aim the clubface at your target. Then open your stance by shifting your feet counterclockwise so that your hips face more toward the target and your toe line points in the direction you want the ball to start. This will allow your hips to turn back less and through more, producing more of an outside-in swing path and the desired fade.

Clubface pointed at your final target, body pointed in the direction you want the ball to start.

THE FADE SWING
Forget where the clubface is aimed and simply swing along your body lines, which due to the open setup will be out and across the target line. Focus on rotating your body a little faster than you normally would and keeping the back of your left hand facing the target at impact. Don't roll your forearms over, because you want to hit the ball with an open clubface. In fact, if you hold off your release you'll finish with the club pointing up and down in your finish like this, which is a good checkpoint.

SHOT 9:
THE PURPOSEFUL DRAW

Curve it to the left to avoid trouble—and add extra yards to boot.

Your approach to the green is blocked by trees on the left and you need to bend the ball around them, or the pin is front left on a fast green and guarded by a large bunker. Or you're on the tee box and there's trouble on the right side of the hole. **Handling these situations calls for a draw, a shot that curves purposely from right to left.**

DIFFICULTY LEVEL

You need a lot of swing speed and an inside-out path—not the beginner's specialty.

SHOT RECIPE

Club:	*Any*
Aim:	*Clubface at target, body lines right*
Stance:	*Aligned more right of your final target*
Ball:	*Standard position*
Swing:	*Full speed*
Feel:	*Longer swing with a full release*

THE DRAW GRIP
Use a stronger hold (hands rotated to the right) and lighter grip pressure. This will help you produce a closed clubface and a drawing ball flight.

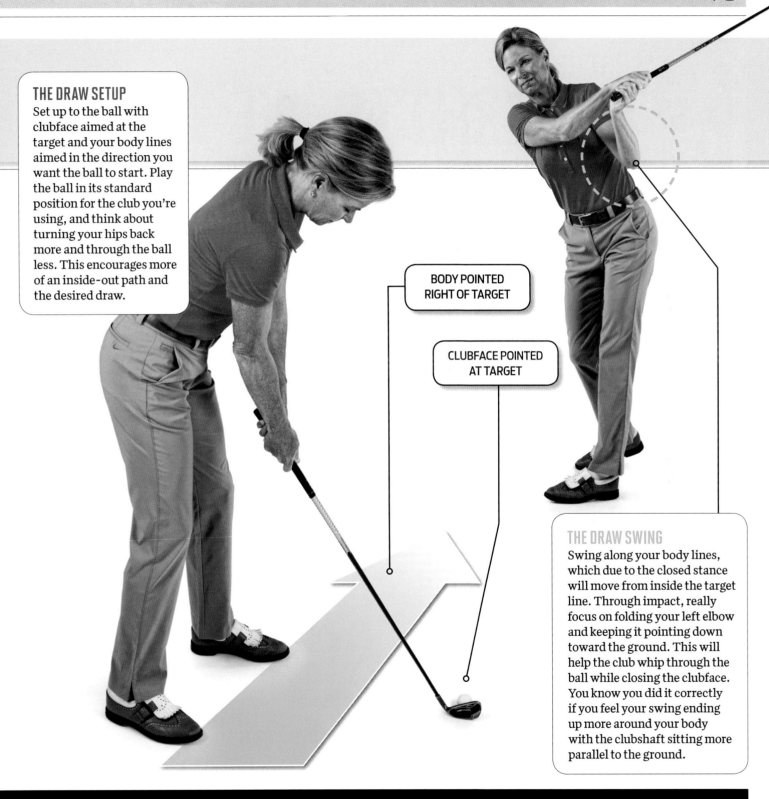

THE DRAW SETUP

Set up to the ball with clubface aimed at the target and your body lines aimed in the direction you want the ball to start. Play the ball in its standard position for the club you're using, and think about turning your hips back more and through the ball less. This encourages more of an inside-out path and the desired draw.

BODY POINTED RIGHT OF TARGET

CLUBFACE POINTED AT TARGET

THE DRAW SWING

Swing along your body lines, which due to the closed stance will move from inside the target line. Through impact, really focus on folding your left elbow and keeping it pointing down toward the ground. This will help the club whip through the ball while closing the clubface. You know you did it correctly if you feel your swing ending up more around your body with the clubshaft sitting more parallel to the ground.

SHOT 10:
THE PERFECT DRIVE

Hitting it long and straight sometimes has more to do with what happens before you swing than it does with the quality of your motion.

Tee-box strategy is a big part of managing the course and your game. The first thing to do as you assess the situation is to consider your natural ball flight. **If you hit a natural draw, you'll want to tee off on the left side of the tee box and aim up the right side of the fairway.** This will allow you to curve the ball almost the full width of the fairway and still be in the short grass. If you hit a natural fade, you'll want to tee up on the right side of the box and aim up the left side of the fairway. These suggestions are a good place to start. Finish your pre-drive planning by following the strategies on these pages.

1. CHECK THE WIND
If you can angle yourself so that you're hitting directly into the wind, then you'll minimize the effects of the breeze. For example, if the wind is blowing left to right, peg the tee in the ground on the right side of the tee box so that when you aim slightly left you're pointed more into the wind, negating its ability to blow the ball off line. Sounds like a bad idea, but it's actually better than dealing with a direct crosswind.

2. TEE AWAY FROM TROUBLE

Tee the ball on the same side as the trouble. This will make it easier for you to avoid any obstacles. In the example here, there's water on the right, so your best play is to tee up on the right side of the box and aim left. This is a bit counterintuitive, but pros do it all the time.

*More tee-box strategies and video lessons on how to add yards to your drives at **golf.com/power** and on the tablet editions of Golf Magazine*

3. LOOK FOR TIGHT SPOTS

Bunkers, trees, water and deep rough need to be avoided at all costs. If you don't have enough room to operate at the distance you normally hit your driver, then throttle back to a 3-wood or hybrid.

4. CHECK YOUR DISTANCES

If a good drive leaves you an awkward distance from the green or too far away to reach it in two shots, then drop down to a 3-wood. Try to position the ball at a comfortable yardage. For example, if your driver gets you to 120 yards and your 3-wood to 150 and you're more comfortable hitting a club that travels 150 yards, then opt for the 3-wood.

SHOT 11:
THE PERFECT PAR-3 SHOT

They're short, but often deadly. Here's what to look for on a par-3 hole to ensure that you make par even if you miss the green.

Even if you only play one course, you need to vary your strategy every day on the par 3s because the ground crew sets the pins in a different position each morning. **As you can guess, club selection is vital.** Is it better to be long or short of the flag? Where are the obstacles to avoid? These are key questions that you need to answer every time you step on the tee box of a par 3.

If the pin is in the very back of the green and there's water behind the hole, choose the club that will only get you as far as the pin, even if you hit it better than you've ever hit it before. If the pin is in the front of the green and just over a bunker, you should select a club that at the very least will carry the bunker, even if you miss it a bit. Although this strategy might put you past the pin in the event you catch the shot flush, it allows you to avoid trouble while giving you a shot at birdie if you hit the green.

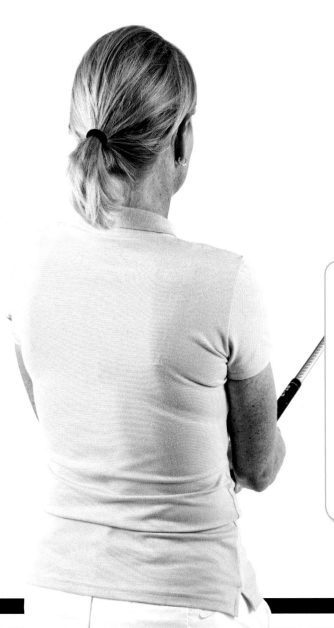

1. PEG IT IN THE RIGHT PLACE

As you decide where to tee your ball on a par 3, the first guideline is to always peg it on the side that limits how much you need to fly the ball over obvious obstacles. Because the pin on this hole is positioned on the left side of the green, your best bet would be to tee up the ball on the right side of the box. From this position you'd only need to carry the right side of the front-left bunker.

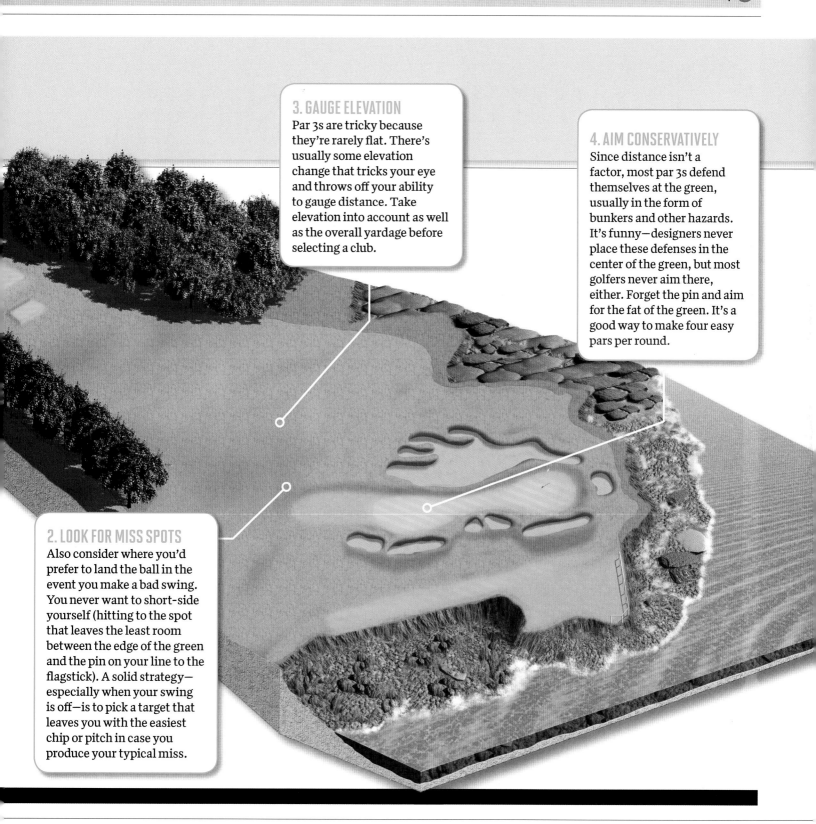

3. GAUGE ELEVATION

Par 3s are tricky because they're rarely flat. There's usually some elevation change that tricks your eye and throws off your ability to gauge distance. Take elevation into account as well as the overall yardage before selecting a club.

4. AIM CONSERVATIVELY

Since distance isn't a factor, most par 3s defend themselves at the green, usually in the form of bunkers and other hazards. It's funny—designers never place these defenses in the center of the green, but most golfers never aim there, either. Forget the pin and aim for the fat of the green. It's a good way to make four easy pars per round.

2. LOOK FOR MISS SPOTS

Also consider where you'd prefer to land the ball in the event you make a bad swing. You never want to short-side yourself (hitting to the spot that leaves the least room between the edge of the green and the pin on your line to the flagstick). A solid strategy—especially when your swing is off—is to pick a target that leaves you with the easiest chip or pitch in case you produce your typical miss.

PART 2: HOW TO FIX YOUR SWING

How to keep 10 of the most common bad shots from ruining your scores.

It's a given that you're going to hit a wayward shot or two when you're out on the course. Even elite players miss. **The key is to keep bad shots from repeating themselves so your scores don't balloon up into the stratosphere.** While there's no substitute for hard work at the range to fix flaws and groove the correct motions presented in this book, there are some secret ways to stem the damage during play and minimize the effects of bad swings. Call them quick fixes, Band-Aids, shortcuts—whatever. On the following pages I'll show you how to adjust your motion on the fly to straighten mis-hits and keep your round motoring toward a good score, even when your swing says otherwise.

FAULT: SHANKING

WHAT IT IS

A ball struck so close to the heel of the club that it actual contacts part of the hosel (the round piece of metal that links the shaft to the clubhead). You know you've hit one if the ball screams immediately low and to the right.

FIX NO. 1: HIT A HYBRID

A ball hit on the heel of a hybrid is much more playable than one hit on the heel of an iron. It will still curve to the right, but not straight right.

FIX NO. 2: PLAY THE BALL OFF THE TOE

One of the main reasons for a shank is swinging too much from the inside, a path that moves the hosel toward your contact point. Pull it back by setting up with the ball played off the toe. Even if you make an inside-out swing, you'll catch the ball flush.

FIX NO. 3: STAND FARTHER AWAY FROM THE BALL

Doing this at address makes it harder to strike the ball toward the heel. It also encourages a more circular swing, which tends to move contact away from the hosel.

More pitch- and chip-shot fixes and expert video lessons at
golf.com/shortgame *and on the tablet editions of* Golf Magazine

FAULT:
SKULLED CHIPS

WHAT IT IS
Instead of sliding the clubhead smoothly under the ball, you strike the middle of the ball with the leading edge of the clubhead, sending it screaming across the green.

FIX:
CHANGE YOUR SETUP
If you're skulling short shots, you're probably crowding the ball at address and standing too upright. Check the photos at right. Regardless of the type of shot you're trying to hit, a good rule of thumb is to always make sure you stand at a distance from the ball that allows your arms to hang naturally from your shoulders.

NO

SKULL SETUP
Because of the delicate nature of chips shots, players tend to stand too close to the ball and squat, thinking this will give them more control. What it does, however, is cramp your swing and prevent your arms from swinging freely under your shoulders. This leads to scooping at impact, which causes the lead edge of the clubhead to swing up into the ball.

YES

SOLID SETUP
Bending forward from your hips so that your chest is over your toes will allow your arms to hang straight down and swing freely under your shoulder line. Tilting correctly from your hips also moves your weight forward and positions your eyes closer to the ground. These adjustments—resulting from a single posture change—make it much easier to contact the ball crisply.

PART 2:
HOW TO FIX YOUR SWING

How to keep 10 of the most common bad shots from ruining your scores.

FAULT:
TOPPED SHOTS

WHAT IT IS
You catch the top half of the ball, usually because you're off balance due to poor posture. I see a lot of amateurs setting up with too much weight over their heels. If your weight is too far back you won't be able to swing on plane. You'll severely mis-hit the ball and come up way short.

FIX NO. 1: GET INTO PROPER POSTURE
Getting back to address position basics can easily turn your top into flush contact.

NO

TOP SETUP
Golfers who squat rather than bend forward tend to lift the club in the backswing to avoid being pulled off balance. This pulls them out of their address posture. Once they rise up their chances of topping the ball skyrocket.

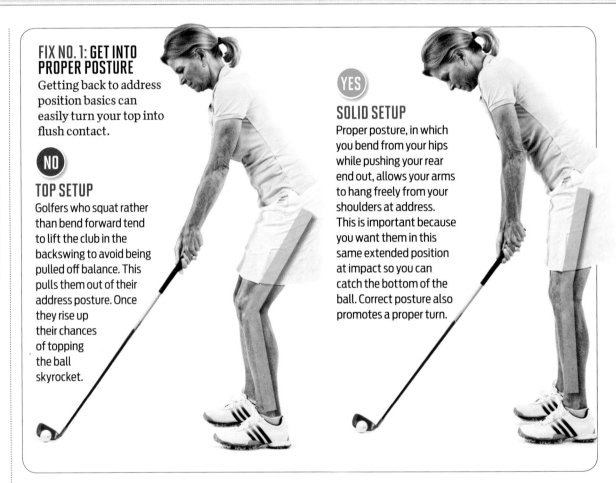

YES

SOLID SETUP
Proper posture, in which you bend from your hips while pushing your rear end out, allows your arms to hang freely from your shoulders at address. This is important because you want them in this same extended position at impact so you can catch the bottom of the ball. Correct posture also promotes a proper turn.

FIX NO. 2: GET YOUR WEIGHT FORWARD
You'll notice that when your posture is correct, your weight is distributed more toward your toes than your heels. An easy check to make sure you're in a solid address is to lift your heels and tap them together. If your setup is off, then you won't be able to smoothly raise your heels because your weight is too far back.

Straighten your right arm to avoid topping.

FIX NO. 3:
STRAIGHTEN YOUR RIGHT ARM

Revisit the downswing arm moves outlined in chapter 2. It's critical that you straighten your right arm on the downswing to get the clubhead all the way down to the ground so you don't top the ball. When you make a backswing, your right elbow folds. To get the club back to the ground in your downswing, you need to re-extend your right arm as if you were throwing the clubhead toward the turf. This straightening also accelerates the clubhead, producing solid contact and more power.

"IT'S CRITICAL THAT YOU STRAIGHTEN YOUR RIGHT ARM ON THE DOWNSWING TO GET THE CLUBHEAD ALL THE WAY DOWN TO THE GROUND SO YOU DON'T TOP THE BALL."

PART 2:
HOW TO FIX YOUR SWING

How to keep 10 of the most common bad shots from ruining your scores.

FAULT: POPPED-UP DRIVES

WHAT IT IS
Instead of flying powerfully down the fairway, your drives shoot straight up into the air. It's the typical poor shot from a player who swings much too steeply into impact. Your goal should be to ascend into impact (i.e., hit slightly up on the ball).

FIX NO. 1: SET UP TO HIT UP

 NO

POP-UP SETUP
Level shoulders at address sounds like a nice idea, but it actually encourages too much of a descending swing—exactly what you don't want when hitting your driver.

 YES

POWER SETUP
Because you want to catch the ball on the upswing (which is why you position the ball past the bottom of your swing arc), tilt your shoulders so that your right one is lower than your left. Notice that if you keep your head centered between your shoulders, your eye line also will tilt. It may feel strange, but it's what you need to produce power.

Connect here.

FIX NO. 2: FLATTEN YOUR SWING
A flatter, rounder, more baseball-style swing will help you sweep the ball off of the tee rather than hit down on it. As you pivot your upper body during your backswing, keep your left arm close to your chest and use the connection to pull your shoulders into action. Practice the right feel by making baseball swings with your driver held parallel to the ground at address, and keep it horizontal both back and through. This more level feeling will get you out of the habit of hitting down and into the habit of swinging up.

FAULT: FAT FAIRWAY WOODS

WHAT IT IS

You're in position to reach a par-5 green in two, but instead of sweeping the ball powerfully off the fairway grass, you drive your club into the turf behind the ball. The resulting divot flies farther than the ball.

FIX: MATCH BALL POSITION TO SWING ARC

The typical mistake is playing the ball too far forward, where you confuse fairway-wood ball position with driver ball position. If you're consistently catching your fairway woods fat, move the ball back till it's slightly left of center. You need to make sure the ball is at the exact point where your swing bottoms out. Use the left side of your face as a guide. This position gives you the best chance to strike the ball at the sweeping point of your swing.

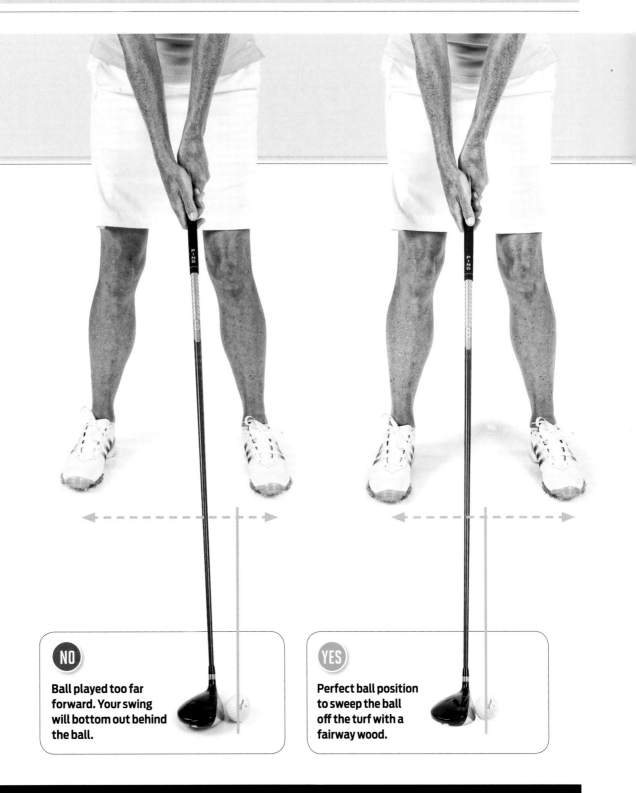

NO
Ball played too far forward. Your swing will bottom out behind the ball.

YES
Perfect ball position to sweep the ball off the turf with a fairway wood.

PART 2:
HOW TO FIX YOUR SWING

How to keep 10 of the most common bad shots from ruining your scores.

FAULT: SLICING

WHAT IT IS
You know what it is: a ball that curves from left to right with little power and the propensity to find trouble on the right side of the course.

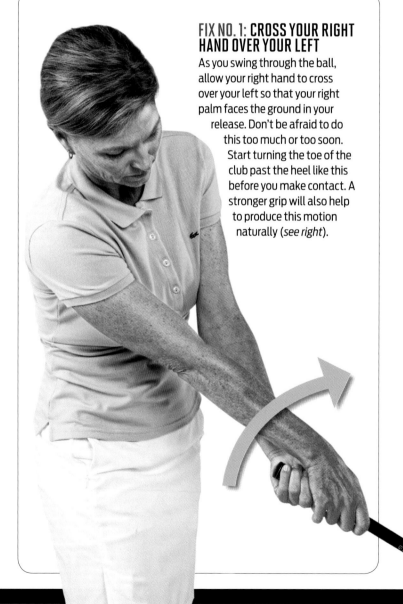

FIX NO. 1: CROSS YOUR RIGHT HAND OVER YOUR LEFT
As you swing through the ball, allow your right hand to cross over your left so that your right palm faces the ground in your release. Don't be afraid to do this too much or too soon. Start turning the toe of the club past the heel like this before you make contact. A stronger grip will also help to produce this motion naturally (*see right*).

FIX NO. 2: PRE-CLOSE THE CLUBFACE
You can slice a ball three ways: 1) with a swing path that's too much outside-in (i.e., across the ball), 2) leaving the clubface open at impact and 3) using a combination of both. If you're having clubface issues, take a stronger grip or close the clubface a few degrees at address by turning the club to the left before you secure your grip. Nothing cures a slice ball flight faster than a closed clubface.

FAULT: HOOKING

WHAT IT IS
A hook is a ball that curves from right to left. You'll get more power with a hook, but like a sliced ball, it also tends to find the worst parts of the course and is very difficult to keep in the air.

FIX NO. 1: PRE-OPEN THE CLUBFACE
You can hook a ball three ways: 1) with a swing path that's too much from inside the target line, 2) unduly closing the clubface at impact and 3) using a combination of both. If you tend to overdo your forearm rotation and close the clubface at impact, open it at address by turning the club to the right before securing your hold. Nothing cures a hook faster than an open clubface.

FIX NO. 2: WEAKEN YOUR GRIP
Weaken your grip by rotating both of your hands to the left. Also, make sure that your right hand completely covers the thumb of your left hand and that the only fingernail you can see is the one on your right thumb. Pinch the grip between your right index finger and thumb to keep your right hand in position and to stop it from rotating over and closing the clubface.

PART 2:
HOW TO FIX YOUR SWING

How to keep 10 of the most common bad shots from ruining your scores.

FAULT: MISSING SHORT PUTTS

Practice with your feet together for better balance and a stroke that stays on line.

WHAT IT IS
A putt you should make, but you pull the ball left or right of the hole.

FIX: PUTT WITH YOUR FEET TOGETHER
You must keep your body completely still in order to sink the short ones. To practice staying steady, putt with your feet together and strive to maintain balance throughout your motion. Putting with your feet together exposes any unwanted movement in your stroke. This will improve your accuracy and distance control.

FAULT: COMING UP SHORT ON LAG PUTTS

WHAT IT IS
While you don't expect to make lengthy putts, you're not lagging them close enough to give yourself a realistic chance of making the next putt.

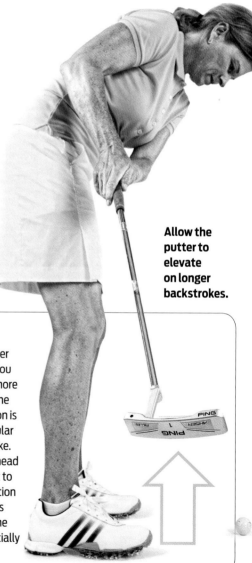

Allow the putter to elevate on longer backstrokes.

FIX: LET IT RISE
A longer putt requires a longer backstroke, and the longer you make your backstroke, the more the putterhead will rise off the ground. This natural elevation is vital to maintaining the circular shape of a solid putting stroke. If you try to keep the putterhead low to the ground from start to finish, you'll lose the connection between your body and arms and make it difficult to roll the ball the right distance, especially from long range.

The moment you give in to your emotions is the moment you can write off any chance of recovering.

FAULT: BAD ATTITUDE

WHAT IT IS

A mental state of mind that allows you to fall victim to your errors instead of overcoming them.

FIXES

Here are my top 10 ways to adjust your attitude when the wheels start to fall off. Use them to be a happier golfer—and a better partner—even when you're not playing your best.

1 Have a reality check. Even great golfers hit bad shots, so expect some misses every time you play. This will keep you from flying off the handle following a poor shot and put you in better position to recover with your next.

2 Keep trying. The round isn't over until you putt out on 18, so don't give up. There's a good chance that you'll figure out your problems if you keep your cool and keep your mind open.

3 Forget distance. Select clubs that are easier to hit, not necessarily the ones that get you on the green with a once-in-lifetime swing. For example, if you're a 3-wood away from the hole, use your 7-wood instead. You're more likely to hit a good shot with a 7-wood and then get down in two than to nail the 3-wood.

4 Breathe and slow down. The tendency is to rush when you're not playing well. This hurry-up-and-get-it-over-with attitude will only make matters worse. Instead, stop and breathe deeply and slowly to clear you head and calm yourself. Then, really start taking your time, making purposeful practice swings and going through your pre-shot routine in its entirety. Pick up the pace only when you rediscover your swing.

5 Use practice swings to your advantage. Don't just make one, make three, and do them in a continuous motion. Often it's something as simple as rhythm that's throwing you off, and making repeated swings can get you back on your natural pace.

6 Use a longer club and a smaller swing. Much like the motion used for a knockdown (*page 172*), a smaller swing makes it easy to get back to making solid contact. If you pair it with a club that's longer than you need, you'll easily reach your target. Try this if you're pressing too much or overswinging.

7 Check your fundamentals. Assess your grip, posture and ball position before making wholesale swing changes. If any of these fundamentals are off, then you won't get back on track even if the rest of your motion is on. Plus, errors here are the easiest to fix.

8 Say less, not more. People often won't notice if you're playing badly if you're composed and not making a spectacle of yourself.

9 Channel your emotions. Use your frustration as a call to action for the future. Let it motivate you to either practice more or seek the help of a qualified teaching professional.

10 Oh well! Say it to yourself, and say it over and over if need be. Keep in mind that there will be other days.

PART 3:
HOW TO PLAY LIKE A PRO

Look and act the part even if you're a beginner.

The old saying, "Fake it till you make it" applies here. While it takes years of experience to learn the gamut of nuances that go into playing the game well, you'll want to fit in and look like you know what you're doing as soon as possible. Doing so will add to your enjoyment of the game and make you a better playing partner—you don't want to be the golfer other players avoid. **Even if your swing is still a work in progress, following the 10 suggestions on these pages will make you look like you're in total control.** Your scores may not be up to par, but your attitude, mindset and playing style will fit in wherever you play.

10 WAYS TO PLAY LIKE A PRO

1 Know what shot to use and when. Learning the different shots that are available to you, what they're called and when it's best to use them will help you manage risk and play beyond your experience.

2 Have a solid setup routine. Concoct a repetitive pre-shot ritual that assembles the key fundamentals of stance, aim, grip, ball position, posture and alignment. Having one makes you more consistent and makes you look like you really know what you're doing.

3 Know your yardages. Getting in touch with how far you hit each of your clubs when you make a solid swing is a must. All good players know what iron to pull from every distance. If you don't, have your professional put together a yardage chart for you and take it with you to the course until you know the numbers by heart.

4 Nail your setup. Your clubs are built to certain specs, and it's important that your setup keeps them intact. Soling a club on the ground sounds simple, but there are nuances to it that you have to keep an eye on. Make sure your clubs sit flat on the ground, not with the toe or heel sections noticeably off the turf. This will set each club at its proper lie angle. Then look for marks to set the club at its proper loft. Most manufacturers add an alignment aid to the club to help you guide it into proper position. Most often this takes the form of a

tick at the bottom of the grip. As you settle into your stance, make sure the tick is pointing straight at you. If it points to the right, then you've gripped the club with the clubface open. If it points to the left, then you've gripped it with the clubface closed. This is especially important when hitting your wedges, with which even a small change in loft can result in a big-time miss.

5 Have a go-to club. Find out which club you consistently hit the best—the one that always comes through in the clutch. Lean on this club on bad days or until you have time to fully work out the kinks.

6 Define your best setup. Know what your ideal grip and posture look like so when you make small mistakes you can self-correct. For example, how many knuckles do you see on your left hand when you're hitting the ball your best? Remember, the correct grip is different for every golfer, so it's imperative that you find yours. Next question: how far is it between you hands and thighs when you bend from your hips with your arms hanging naturally? Once you know the distance, make sure you nail it when you set up, no matter which club you're using. Take a look at stance width and ball position, too.

7 Learn the lingo and the basic rules. A golfer sounds like a golfer. You can learn the proper terminology by watching golf on

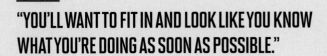

"YOU'LL WANT TO FIT IN AND LOOK LIKE YOU KNOW WHAT YOU'RE DOING AS SOON AS POSSIBLE."

television, reading books and magazines or by hanging around the clubhouse. And buy a rules book. You'll be surprised how deeply they affect everyday play.

8 **Get out and play.** Experience pays off. When you play with other golfers you can learn just by watching how they move around the course. The more experienced the player, the better the model he or she will be for your game.

9 **Learn distance control with your short game.** Once you know the basic short shots and have reached a moderate level of proficiency in making solid contact with each of your wedges, focus on how far you hit them and how to dial in yardages by either switching clubs or modifying your swing. Spend some time on the range hitting different shots with different wedges and with different-size swings, then log the results in a notebook. You can save a lot of strokes and look like a player when your short-game approach shots roll right next to the hole.

10 **Get the right gear.** Playing with clubs that allow you to take advantage of your natural swing shape and swing speed is the only way you'll reach your true scoring potential. When the specs on your clubs don't match what you need, you'll have a difficult time controlling distance and direction. At the very least, have your gear checked for proper spacing (an equal number of degrees between each of your irons), and make sure you're carrying the right mix of woods, hybrids and irons. In the long run, however, you'll need a custom fitting to perform at your absolute best.

WHAT TO DO WHEN YOU'RE IN A BUNKER

Your goal in greenside sand is to get the ball out—on your first swing. Here's how to do it step-by step and make sure your next shot is a putt.

THE EASY WAY TO
ESCAPE THE SAND

INSIDE
Three ways to learn the basics you need:

LESSONS
Tips and instruction to help you master fundamental moves and positions

CHECKPOINTS
Tests to see if you're keeping up or falling behind in your quest to build a better game

DRILLS
Practice tips and step-by-step exercises to make new moves second nature

The bunker shot is different from all others in golf. It's the only one in which it's perfectly okay to miss the ball.

Given a choice, Tour players would almost always prefer to play from greenside sand than from the rough. The reason is simple: pros can spin the ball much easier—and stop it quicker—from sand than they can chipping or pitching it from the rough. Recreational golfers, however, would prefer anything to sand. They're about as comfortable playing a shot from the beach as they are hitting over water or swimming among a school of sharks.

The standard greenside bunker shot is one of the scariest shots for amateurs for several reasons. First and foremost, they don't understand what the club is designed to do in the sand—which is to slide, not dig. They're also unsure of what adjustments to make to their basic setup and swing technique compared with a similar-length wedge shot from a normal or grassy lie in the fairway. Last of all, they

don't practice the shot, opting generally to hit a few putts or drives instead before they head to the first tee. Indeed, the practice bunker at any course or range is a very lonely place. In the event amateurs do practice sand shots, they do so with an emphasis on the ball and not the interaction between the clubhead and the sand. Learning how to slide the clubhead through the sand is paramount for success.

What separates the greenside bunker shot from every other shot in golf is that the clubhead doesn't contact the ball; rather, the ball moves out on a pillow of sand. In other words, the ball is just along for the ride. Once you grasp this concept and learn to slide the clubhead through the sand and hit the correct entry point, bunker play becomes much easier. There are some other variables to learn, such as how to control the distance of your bunker shots and how to adjust to sloping lies, but the primary goal remains the same: hit a spot on the sand a few inches behind the ball and slide the clubhead under the ball. Once you get part of the equation down, you can make slight adjustments to your setup and swing to really get the ball close from a variety of lies.

"ONCE YOU LEARN TO SLIDE THE CLUB THROUGH THE SAND AND HIT THE CORRECT ENTRY POINT, BUNKER PLAY BECOMES MUCH EASIER."

YOUR BUNKER BUSTER

MIKE DAVIS
Walters Golf Academy,
Royal Links Golf Club, Las Vegas, Nev.
Golf Magazine Top 100 Teacher (2007–present)
● 16-time PGA Teacher of the Year (Pacific Northwest and Southwest Sections, Southern Nevada and Oregon Chapters)
● PGA President's Council on Growing the Game (2008, 2010)
● PGA Tour member in mid-1970s (3 U.S. Open appearances; 1 PGA)
● Teaching since 1971
www.mikedavisgolf.net

THE PRIMARY KEY:
SLIDE, DON'T DIG

The clubhead should never make contact with the ball, only the sand.

Gene Sarazen was the first player to win all four major championships (Masters, U.S. Open, British Open and PGA Championship), a feat that later came to be known as the Career Grand Slam. But perhaps his greatest contribution to golf was the invention of the sand wedge in the early 1930s. Sarazen added lead to the bottom of a niblick (an iron with a big, heavy head and flat, narrow sole), bulking up the flange so that the clubhead's trailing edge sat well below the leading edge. In the process, he added loft and bounce (i.e., the angle between the leading edge and trailing edge), making it possible to slide the clubhead through the sand, under the ball, and drive the ball up and out of the bunker on a much higher, softer trajectory. By adding bounce to his club, Sarazen revolutionized bunker play, making it much easier for every golfer since to lift the ball out of the bunker and stop it dead on the green.

Prior to the invention of the sand wedge, golfers had to pick the ball cleanly or attempt to skim the surface of the sand, and do so with a club that was designed to dig. What Sarazen's wedge did was enable the club to glide through the sand rather than burrow in the bunker, providing golfers with a sense of control. With the right equipment, golfers could be more aggressive from the sand and not only get the ball out of the bunker, but consistently land it close to the hole.

To be a good bunker player, you must learn how to slide the clubhead through the sand without contacting the ball. **Moreover, you need to establish consistent entry and exit points.** The better you are at controlling the path of the clubhead through the sand and under the ball, the easier time you'll have escaping bunkers in one swing.

> "YOU'VE GOT TO LEARN HOW TO SLIDE THE CLUB THROUGH THE SAND WITHOUT CONTACTING THE BALL."

HOW TO GROOVE THE RIGHT PATH.

Use this drill to create the perfect divot every time.

STEP 1

Draw two lines in the sand about 10 to 12 inches apart, perpendicular to your target line. You don't need a ball for this drill.

NO
NOT HERE
If the clubhead enters the sand either before or past the first line, or the divot is too deep or shallow, then continue to perform the drill without a ball until you can consistently carve the proper-size divot between the two lines.

TARGET

YES
HIT HERE
The clubhead should enter the sand at the first line and exit at the second. The depth and length of the divot will vary depending on the texture of the sand; shallower and shorter in hard sand, and deeper and longer in soft sand. As you gain experience, enter the sand closer to the ball for greater spin and distance, and farther away from the ball for less spin and distance.

YES / TARGET

STEP 2

Swinging your sand wedge, see if you can hit the first line and slide the clubhead through the sand to the second line. Once you can go from line to line on a consistent basis (at least five in a row), add a ball (*below left*) and repeat the drill. If you do it correctly the ball will pop out nice and softly. Keep in mind that the ball is just along for the ride; the sand is what propels it up and outward. Not only must you become efficient at controlling the entry and exit points, but also at managing how the clubhead slides through the sand.

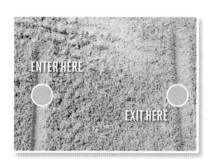

ENTER HERE / EXIT HERE

CHART YOUR PROGRESS

How to Escape the Sand
- ☑ *The basic key*
- ❑ *How to set up*
- ❑ *How to swing*
- ❑ *Adjust for distance and sand type*
- ❑ *Adjust for lies and slopes*

HOW TO NAIL YOUR
SAND SETUP

Set up to ensure that you hit the sand first, behind the ball.

Since the goal for most greenside bunker shots is to hit a specific spot in the sand behind the ball (and not the ball itself), the setup is a bit different from your standard iron shot. Instead of having your hands ahead of the ball and the shaft leaning toward the target (a sure way to hit a rocket from the sand), **play the ball forward in your stance, with your head, spine and hands directly over the spot you want to impact in the sand** (i.e., three to four inches behind the ball in normal sand). These adjustments alone should guarantee sand-first contact.

It's also advisable to take a weaker grip, with your left thumb and the "V" formed by your right thumb and index finger more on top of the handle. This creates a slightly cupped left-wrist position, which exposes the bounce (more on this shortly), opens the clubface and encourages the clubface to remain open through impact and slide through the sand. If the clubface closes, then the clubhead will dig too much. The only thing you want digging into the sand is your feet, which will help with stability.

How much you open or close the clubface at address depends on the length of the shot and the texture of the sand. On longer shots, you should square or close the face and have a shallower angle of attack, whereas on shorter ones you should open the face and have a steeper angle of attack.

HANDS
The shaft should be fairly vertical, with your hands and clubhead hanging directly over the club's point of entry in the sand. The correct posture, grip and hand position make it much easier to slide the clubhead through the sand.

FEET
Dig your feet into the bunker so the soles of your shoes are under the surface of the sand. This not only helps with stability, but it also moves the bottom of your swing arc under the ball, which helps remove the fear of skulling the ball.

BOUNCE ANGLE

LEAD EDGE

BOUNCE FACTOR

The angle between the sole's leading and trailing edges is known as the bounce. It creates an upward force to offset the downward force of the clubface, allowing the clubhead to glide through the sand. My sand wedge (*pictured here*) has 58 degrees of loft and 12 degrees of bounce. Most 56-degree wedges start with 8 degrees of bounce and run as high as 16 degrees. The greater the bounce, the more the club will resist digging. Opening the clubface at address (pointing right of your target line) increases the bounce angle even more. The softer and fluffier the sand, the more you want to open the face and expose the bounce so the club doesn't encounter as much resistance.

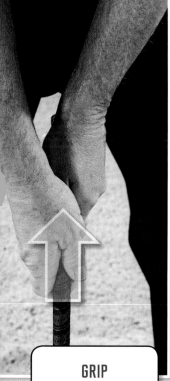

GRIP

Weaken your grip (hands turned counterclockwise) so the "V's" formed by your thumbs and index fingers on both hands are on top of the grip. A weaker grip helps to keep the clubface open, so it slides, rather than digs, through the sand.

NO

SHAFT LEAN

Setting up with your hands forward and shaft leaning toward the target encourages ball-first contact and negates the bounce of your wedge.

CHART YOUR PROGRESS

How to Escape the Sand

☑ The basic key
☑ How to set up
☐ How to swing
☐ Adjust for distance and sand type
☐ Adjust for lies and slopes

HOW TO MAKE A
SOLID SAND SWING

Here are a few swing thoughts for developing a consistent entry point in the sand.

You don't need power to hit good bunker shots you need precision. A steady head provides just that, as it ensures that the clubhead takes a consistent path through the sand. If your upper body moves up and down or side to side too much during your swing, then the club's entry point in the sand will be all over the place and you'll have a tough time controlling your bunker shots.

HOW TO DO IT

See that your head, chin, navel, hands and clubhead all form a straight line, directly over your impact point (i.e., point of entry in the sand). Since it's too much to think about all of these different parts, **focus on keeping your chin on top of the impact point as you swing back and through.** Provided your chin is over the correct entry point in the sand, you'll not only impact the sand in the proper place every time, but the path the clubhead travels through the sand will go underneath and past the ball. (The club's entry point in the sand varies based on the texture of the sand: three to four inches for normal sand, two to three inches for hard sand, and three to six inches for soft sand.) This is necessary to carve the correct path through the sand regardless of its texture or density.

CHART YOUR PROGRESS

How to Escape the Sand	☑	The basic key
	☑	How to set up
	☑	How to swing
	❑	Adjust for distance and sand type
	❑	Adjust for lies and slopes

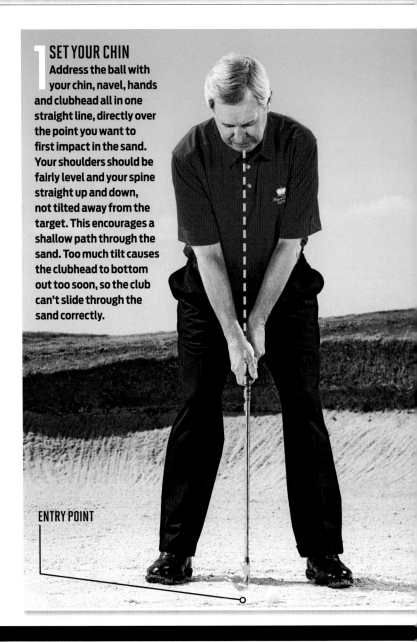

1 SET YOUR CHIN
Address the ball with your chin, navel, hands and clubhead all in one straight line, directly over the point you want to first impact in the sand. Your shoulders should be fairly level and your spine straight up and down, not tilted away from the target. This encourages a shallow path through the sand. Too much tilt causes the clubhead to bottom out too soon, so the club can't slide through the sand correctly.

ENTRY POINT

2 HOLD IT STEADY

As you swing back, keep your head steady so that your chin remains directly over the entry point. Your shoulders should turn some, but not as much as they would in a full swing. There should also be very little weight shift onto your right foot. Your left wrist should be cupped at the top, which helps you to slide the clubhead under the ball.

ENTRY POINT

3 SLIDE THROUGH

Hit the impact point and slide the club through the sand. You should have the feeling that the left wrist is cupped and the clubhead is passing your hands early so you can slide it underneath the ball. The wrist action is similar to what you would experience in a flop shot since you want the clubface to remain open through impact.

ENTRY POINT

HOW TO PLAY FROM
HARD OR SOFT SAND

Soft and fluffy? Hard as cement? Knowing how to adjust your setup and swing is the key to handling different textures of sand.

All sand isn't alike. Some courses feature soft, fluffy sand that you can sink your feet several inches into, while others feature sand as hard as an airport runway. In the latter case, it's very easy to bounce the club off the firm surface and catch the shot thin, while in the former instance you have to guard against digging the clubhead too far underneath the ball. Dry and sugary, or wet and compact, **you need to know how to adjust your setup and technique so that you can take the right amount of sand and make a clean escape.**

You don't want to head to Scotland or Ireland without any idea of how to play from firm bunkers, just as you don't want to plan a golf vacation in the Caribbean or some other exotic place without a clue how to tame fluffy lies. The following keys will prepare you for both conditions. Practice both to get a feel for what is needed for each texture of sand.

HARD SAND
LESS BOUNCE, STEEPER APPROACH

SETUP
Set up with the ball back of center in your stance and your weight favoring your front side, which promotes a steeper angle of attack into the ball. The shaft should lean toward the target, with your hands slightly ahead of the ball. Square or close the clubface to reduce the amount of bounce and encourage more of a digging action through the sand.

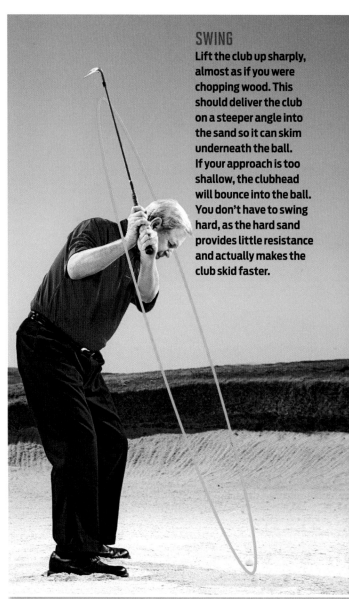

SWING
Lift the club up sharply, almost as if you were chopping wood. This should deliver the club on a steeper angle into the sand so it can skim underneath the ball. If your approach is too shallow, the clubhead will bounce into the ball. You don't have to swing hard, as the hard sand provides little resistance and actually makes the club skid faster.

SOFT SAND
MORE BOUNCE, SHALLOWER APPROACH

SETUP

In soft sand, the angle of attack must be shallower, and you need more bounce on the sole so that the club doesn't dig into the sand too much. Position the ball forward of center in your stance and open the clubface to expose the bounce and make it easier to slide the clubhead through the sand. Your shoulders should be tilted slightly away from the target, with both hands behind the ball and under your chin.

SWING

On your backswing, rotate your chest and shoulders so that the club swings more around your body, which promotes the shallower plane you need to prevent the clubhead from digging into and burrowing in the sand. Swing faster than you would from a normal lie, as the soft sand tends to resist more, making it difficult to slide the clubhead through it.

HOW TO BLAST IT
SHORTER OR LONGER

Short, medium or long, these setup and swing adjustments will have you locked in on the correct distance to the flag.

The major key to becomming an elite bunker player and increasing your sand-save percentage is controlling how far you hit your bunker shots from different types of sand. **The easiest way to hit the ball longer or shorter is by adjusting the following: 1) the speed of your swing, 2) the loft on the clubface or 3) the club's angle of attack into the sand.** Ball position plays a huge part in the latter, but if you need to take a few yards off to get at that tight pin location, or carry the ball 10 yards farther to get at those tough-to-reach back hole locations, these three distance adjustments ought to serve you well. A balance of swing speed, loft and angle of attack is what you need to control your shots. Here's a closer look at each.

DISTANCE FACTOR NO. 1
SWING SPEED

Swing harder for longer shots, easier for shorter shots. This comes with the caveat that if you swing too hard you can struggle with inconsistency, and if you swing too easy the clubhead may get stuck in the sand. But everything being equal, more speed means more distance. Don't consciously attempt to control the length of each swing; instead, try to feel the amount of swing needed for each distance, similar to putting. The swing should be smooth and even paced.

DISTANCE FACTOR NO. 2
LOFT

You can add loft by either opening the clubface (rotating it clockwise so the grooves point more toward the sky) or going to a higher-lofted club, and decrease loft by squaring, or closing, the face or taking a less-lofted club, such as a 9-iron. The latter strategy is often used on long bunker shots—25 yards or more—since it allows you to make a normal swing (for a shot of that distance).

Escape any bunker with the help of dozens of video lessons at **golf.com/sand** *and on the tablet editions of Golf Magazine*

DISTANCE FACTOR NO. 3 ANGLE OF ATTACK

A steeper angle of attack produces a more vertical force, resulting in less distance. A shallower angle of attack does just the opposite and directs the force of the swing toward the target to generate more distance. To steepen your angle of attack, move the ball back in your stance so that your hands are ahead of the ball and lift the club up on a more vertical plane during your backswing. For a shallower angle of attack, move the ball forward and make a wider, rounder swing.

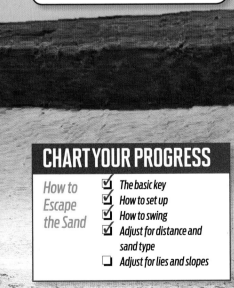

CHART YOUR PROGRESS

How to Escape the Sand

- ☑ The basic key
- ☑ How to set up
- ☑ How to swing
- ☑ Adjust for distance and sand type
- ☐ Adjust for lies and slopes

SHORT, MEDIUM AND LONG ADJUSTMENTS

The density of the sand (i.e., hard or soft) will dictate how to apply the adjustments (*left*) to create the desired distance for your bunker shot.

Steep angle

Normal angle

Shallow angle

		Short Shot (10–15 yds)	Medium Shot (15–25 yds)	Long Shot (25+ yds)
HARD SAND	**Ball Position**	Back	Slightly back	Normal
	Swing Shape	Very steep	Steep	Normal
	Swing Speed	Easier	Normal	Faster
	Clubface	Square/closed	Square	Square/open
SOFT SAND	**Ball Position**	Normal	Slightly forward	Forward
	Swing Shape	Normal	Shallower	Very shallow
	Swing Speed	Normal	Faster	Very fast
	Clubface	Very open	Open	Normal (less-lofted club)

Open clubface

Square clubface

Ball forward

Ball back

HOW TO ESCAPE
FROM BURIED LIES

The leading edge of the club holds the key to excavating the ball from these trouble lies.

A buried lie offers a stiff challenge to even the best players in the world. Since the ball is at least partially submerged in the sand, it's next to impossible to get any backspin on the ball, which causes it to roll out much farther. These shots are hard to control, and in many cases are just like being tagged with a one-stroke penalty.

For the average golfer, there's nothing wrong with needing three shots to get the ball up and down from a buried, semi-buried or fried-egg lie. The goal is to simply get the ball out anywhere on the putting surface so that you can two-putt and move on to the next hole having suffered minimal damage.

When playing these shots, close the clubface on your sand or lob wedge or use a pitching wedge or gap wedge with a smaller sole and less bounce than the typical sand wedge. The key to blasting from any kind of buried lie is getting the leading edge of the club under the ball. This is more difficult with a sand wedge since the bounce on the sole is designed to resist digging. Try the following methods in practice to help you with these three nasty lies.

BURIED AND SEMI-BURIED LIES

Set up with most of your weight on your left side and the ball positioned in the middle of your stance. Close the face of your sand or pitching wedge so that it can dig more easily through the sand. Pick the club up sharply on the backswing and then drive the leading edge of the clubhead hard into the sand, far enough behind the ball to get the leading edge underneath it. You should feel as if you're trying to scoop the ball up and out of the sand, just as if you were scooping some ice cream out of a container. Provided you get the leading edge deep enough under the ball, the scooping action should create a vertical explosion of sand that pops the ball out and onto the green.

1 SEMI-BURIED
At least half of the ball sits below the surface of the sand.

2 BURIED
At least three-quarters of the ball sits below the surface of the sand.

ALTERNATIVE METHOD

Realistically, you can't do much more with a ball in a fried-egg lie than dislodge it, but that's about all you have to do. In fact, you're free to commit the most common bunker error of all time and quit on the shot. More good news? You get to make a violent, no-finish swing and pound that stupid bunker!

Make a full backswing, then slam the club powerfully into the sand an inch or two behind and beneath your ball as if you're trying to bury the clubhead. Don't expect any follow-through, just a soft rebound effect as your club emerges lazily from the sand. Meanwhile your ball and a divot of sand are already crossing the bunker lip on their way to the green.

FRIED-EGG LIE

You'll see this lie frequently on courses with very dry, fluffy sand. The ball lands with a thud, carving out a crater and creating a ridge of surroung all the way around it, similar to an egg white surrounding its yoke. You want to employ the same technique as the buried lie shot, scooping underneath the ball instead of sliding the club through the sand. The difference is that you want the leading edge to enter the sand farther behind the ball, at the edge of the crater. For this reason, you may want to play the ball slightly forward of center in your stance. The only way to improve from these trouble lies is to practice and learn the interaction between the club and the sand so you can feel what adjustments will work in each situation.

FRIED EGG
The ball sits smack in the middle of the depression it made when it impacted the sand.

"THE GOAL WITH THE FIRST SHOT IS TO SIMPLY GET THE BALL OUT ANYWHERE ON THE PUTTING SURFACE SO THAT YOU CAN TWO-PUTT AND MOVE ON TO THE NEXT HOLE."

CHART YOUR PROGRESS

How to Escape the Sand

- ☑ The basic key
- ☑ How to set up
- ☑ How to swing
- ☑ Adjust for distance and sand type
- ☑ Adjust for lies and slopes

HOW TO
BLAST FROM SLOPING LIES

Uneven lies pop up just as much in a bunker as they do on the fairway. Adjusting your posture so that it matches the slope is the key to making a clean escape.

In any greenside bunker situation, you want to match the shape of your swing to the slope you're standing on. Otherwise you're going to have a hard time sliding the clubhead underneath the ball.

For example, if the ball is below your feet and you don't adjust your body to the slope, you're going to miss the ball entirely or hit a thin tracer over the green. **Adjusting your posture to match the slope, whether it's uphill or downhill or tilted from left to right or right to left, is the key to getting out in one shot and saving yourself a stroke or two.**

To manage these slippery slopes, it's also very important to understand how the slope affects both the trajectory and direction of the shot. Here are the four most common uneven lies you'll find in the bunker and the adjustments you need to make for each to hit your impact point and slide the club through the sand.

BALL ABOVE YOUR FEET
Stand a little taller than normal to match the slope and ensure that you don't hit the shot too fat. Also make sure to aim to the right to allow for the amount the clubface points left (due to the ball being above your feet and the loft on the clubface). The face angle is responsible for 80 percent of the ball's starting direction, which is why it's important to aim right in this instance.

UPHILL LIE
Take a much wider stance than normal for balance and tilt your body to match the slope. Your chin, navel, hands and club should all form a perpendicular line to the sand, just as they would with a level lie. Swing a little harder than normal to allow for the higher launch angle the slope will create. If the slope is really severe, drop down a club (i.e., use a pitching wedge instead of a sand wedge).

CONCLUDING THOUGHTS: PRACTICE LIKE THE PROS

The gap in skill between the Tour pro and the average golfer may be greatest in the greenside bunker. Give any Tour player a decent lie in the bunker and a little green to work with and he'll get the ball up and down more than 75 percent of the time. They make it look easy because they understand the basics. The average golfer, because he or she doesn't understand what the wedge is designed to do or how to slide the clubhead under the ball, makes it more complicated than necessary.

It's no coincidence that the Tour pros also practice a lot more out of the bunker than amateurs do. They spend the vast majority of their practice time working on their short game, not hitting drive after drive on the range. With a basic understanding of technique and a concentrated effort to practice more from the sand, you can improve your performance from the bunkers. In fact, there's no reason why you can't become every bit as consistent from the bunker as the pros are.

The real key to hitting better sand shots is practice.

BALL BELOW YOUR FEET

Bend over more from your hips to match the slope and aim to the left to allow for the amount the clubface points to the right. Dig your feet a little deeper into the sand to help with your balance and do your best to stay down through the shot, maintaining your address posture (i.e., spine angle) from start to finish.

DOWNHILL LIE

Take a much wider stance than normal to help with your balance and tilt your body so that your spine is perpendicular to the slope. As you slide the clubhead underneath the ball, you should have the feeling it's chasing the ball down the hill. The ball will come out lower, so expect it to run more. If the lie is really severe, don't play toward the hole. Opt for a safer and easier shot.

THE TOP 100 TEACHERS IN AMERICA

There are more than 36,000 PGA and LPGA of America members, and Golf Magazine uses only the 100 most elite among them to help you lower your scores, improve your swing, hammer the ball longer and putt the lights out.

MIKE ADAMS
Facility: Hamilton Farm G.C., Gladstone, N.J.; The Medalist Club, Hobe Sound, Fla.
Website: mikeadamsgolf.com
Teaching since: 1977
Top 100 since: 1996

ROB AKINS
Facility: Spring Creek Ranch, Collierville, Tenn.
Website: robakinsgolf.com
Teaching since: 1987
Top 100 since: 2001

ERIC ALPENFELS
Facility: Pinehurst Resort, Pinehurst, N.C.
Website: pinehurst.com
Teaching since: 1984
Top 100 since: 2001

TODD ANDERSON
Facility: Sea Island Golf Learning Center, St. Simons Island, Ga.
Website: seaisland.com
Teaching since: 1984
Top 100 since: 2003
2010 PGA Teacher of the Year

ROBERT BAKER
Facility: Logical Golf, Miami Beach, Fla.
Website: logicalgolf.com
Teaching since: 1989
Top 100 since: 1999

JIMMY BALLARD
Facility: Ballard Swing Connection, Key Largo, Fla.
Website: jimmyballardgolf.com
Teaching since: 1960
Top 100 since: 1996

MIKE BENDER
Facility: Magnolia Plantation G.C., Lake Mary, Fla.
Website: mikebender.com
Teaching since: 1990
Top 100 since: 1996
2009 PGA Teacher of the Year

STEVE BOSDOSH
Facility: Members Club at Four Streams, Beallsville, Md.
Website: stevebosdoshgolf.com
Teaching since: 1983
Top 100 since: 2001

MICHAEL BREED
Facility: Sunningdale C.C., Scarsdale, N.Y.
Website: michaelbreed.com
Teaching since: 1986
Top 100 since: 2003

BRAD BREWER
Facility: Brad Brewer Golf Academy at Shingle Creek Resort, Orlando, Fla.
Website: bradbrewer.com
Teaching since: 1984
Top 100 since: 2007

HENRY BRUNTON
Facility: Henry Brunton Golf Academy, Maple, Ont.
Website: henrybrunton.com
Teaching since: 1985
Top 100 since: 2005

JASON CARBONE
Facility: Baltusrol G.C., Springfield, N.J.
Teaching since: 1993
Top 100 since: 2007

CHUCK COOK
Facility: Chuck Cook Golf Academy, Austin, Texas
Website: chuckcookgolf.com
Teaching since: 1975
Top 100 since: 1996
1996 PGA Teacher of the Year

DONALD CRAWLEY
Facility: Boulders Golf Academy, Carefree, Ariz.
Website: golfsimplified.com
Teaching since: 1974
Top 100 since: 1999

MIKE DAVIS
Facility: Walters Golf Academy, Las Vegas, Nev.
Website: mikedavisgolf.net
Teaching since: 1971
Top 100 since: 2007

GLENN DECK
Facility: Pelican Hill Resort, Newport Beach, Calif.
Website: pelicanhill.com
Teaching since: 1983
Top 100 since: 2003

DOM DiJULIA
Facility: Dom DiJulia School of Golf, New Hope, Pa.
Website: dijuliagolf.com
Teaching since: 1989
Top 100 since: 2007

KRISTA DUNTON
Facility: Berkeley Hall, Bluffton, S.C.
Website: kristadunton.com
Teaching since: 1989
Top 100 since: 2011
2002 LPGA Teacher of the Year

JOHN ELLIOTT, JR.
Facility: Golden Ocala Golf and Equestrian Club, Ocala, Fla.
Website: jmegolf.com
Teaching since: 1970
Top 100 since: 1996

CHUCK EVANS
Facility: Gold Canyon Golf Resort, Gold Canyon, Ariz.
Website: medicusgolfinstitute.com
Teaching since: 1970
Top 100 since: 2009

BILL FORREST
Facility: Troon C.C., Scottsdale, Ariz.
Website: billforrestgolf.com
Teaching since: 1978
Top 100 since: 2007
2006 PGA Teacher of the Year

EDEN FOSTER
Facility: Maidstone Club, East Hampton, N.Y.
Teaching since: 1988
Top 100 since: 2003

BRYAN GATHRIGHT
Facility: Oak Hills C.C., San Antonio, Texas
Teaching since: 1987
Top 100 since: 2001

DAVID GLENZ
Facility: David Glenz Golf Academy, Franklin, N.J.
Website: davidglenz.com
Teaching since: 1978
Top 100 since: 1996
1998 PGA Teacher of the Year

RICK GRAYSON
Facility: Rivercat G.C., Springfield, Mo.
Website: rickgraysongolf.com
Teaching since: 1976
Top 100 since: 1996

FRED GRIFFIN
Facility: Grand Cypress Academy of Golf, Orlando, Fla.
Website: grandcypress.com
Teaching since: 1980
Top 100 since: 1996

RON GRING
Facility: Gring Golf at Timber Creek G.C., Daphne, Ala.
Website: gringgolf.com
Teaching since: 1978
Top 100 since: 2003

LOU GUZZI
Facility: Lou Guzzi Golf Academy, Talamore C.C., Ambler, Pa.
Website: louguzzi.com
Teaching since: 1992
Top 100 since: 2011

MARK HACKETT
Facility: Old Palm G.C., Palm Beach Gardens, Fla.
Teaching since: 1988
Top 100 since: 2009

MARTIN HALL
Facility: Ibis Golf & C.C., West Palm Beach, Fla.
Teaching since: 1978
Top 100 since: 1996
2008 PGA Teacher of the Year

JOE HALLETT
Facility: Vanderbilt Legends Club, Franklin, Tenn.
Website: pgaguy.com
Teaching since: 1990
Top 100 since: 2011

HANK HANEY
Facility: Hank Haney Golf, McKinney, Texas
Website: hankhaney.com
Teaching since: 1977
Top 100 since: 1996

JIM HARDY
Facility: Jim Hardy Golf, Houston, Texas
Website: jimhardygolf.com
Teaching since: 1966
Top 100 since: 1996
2007 PGA Teacher of the Year

BUTCH HARMON, JR.
Facility: Butch Harmon School of Golf, Henderson, Nev.
Website: butchharmon.com
Teaching since: 1965
Top 100 since: 1996

CRAIG HARMON
Facility: Oak Hill C.C., Rochester, N.Y.
Teaching since: 1968
Top 100 since: 1996

MICHAEL HEBRON
Facility: Smithtown Landing G.C., Smithtown, N.Y.
Website: mikehebron.com
Teaching since: 1967
Top 100 since: 1996
1991 PGA Teacher of the Year

SHAWN HUMPHRIES
Facility: Cowboys G.C., Grapevine, Texas
Website: shawnhumphries.com
Teaching since: 1988
Top 100 since: 2005

ED IBARGUEN
Facility: Duke University G.C., Durham, N.C.
Website: golf.duke.edu
Teaching since: 1979
Top 100 since: 2001

ERIC JOHNSON
Facility: Oakmont C.C., Oakmont, Pa.
Website: ericjohnsongolf.com
Teaching since: 1991
Top 100 since: 2011

HANK JOHNSON
Facility: Greystone G.C., Birmingham, Ala.
Teaching since: 1970
Top 100 since: 1999
2004 PGA Teacher of the Year

CHARLIE KING
Facility: Reynolds Golf Academy, Greensboro, Ga.
Website: reynoldsgolfacademy.com
Teaching since: 1989
Top 100 since: 2003

JERRY KING
Facility: Kapalua Golf Academy, Lahaina, Maui, Hawaii
Website: jerrykinggolf.com
Teaching since: 1992
Top 100 since: 2009

PETER KOSTIS
Facility: Kostis/McCord Learning Center, Scottsdale, Ariz.
Website: kostismccordlearning.com
Teaching since: 1971
Top 100 since: 1996

PETER KRAUSE
Facility: Hank Haney Academy, Lewisville, Texas
Website: peterkrausegolf.com
Teaching since: 1981
Top 100 since: 1999
2005 PGA Teacher of the Year

MIKE LaBAUVE
Facility: Westin Kierland Resort, Scottsdale, Ariz.
Website: kierlandresort.com
Teaching since: 1980
Top 100 since: 1996

ROD LIDENBERG
Facility: Prestwick G.C., Woodbury, Minn.
Website: pgamasterpro.com
Teaching since: 1972
Top 100 since: 2007

JACK LUMPKIN
Facility: Sea Island Golf Learning Center, St. Simons Island, Ga.
Website: seaisland.com
Teaching since: 1958
Top 100 since: 1996
1995 PGA Teacher of the Year

KEITH LYFORD
Facility: Golf Academy at Old Greenwood, Truckee, Calif.
Website: lyfordgolf.net
Teaching since: 1982
Top 100 since: 1999

TIM MAHONEY
Facility: Talking Stick G.C., Scottsdale, Ariz.
Website: timmahoneygolf.com
Teaching since: 1980
Top 100 since: 1996

MIKE MALASKA
Facility: Superstition Mountain G.C., Apache Junction, Ariz.
Website: malaskagolf.com
Teaching since: 1982
Top 100 since: 1996
2011 PGA Teacher of the Year

BRIAN MANZELLA
Facility: English Turn Golf & C.C., New Orleans, La.
Website: brianmanzella.com
Teaching since: 1989
Top 100 since: 2011

PAUL MARCHAND
Facility: Shadowhawk G.C., Richmond, Tex.
Teaching since: 1981
Top 100 since: 1996

LYNN MARRIOTT
Facility: Legacy Golf Resort, Phoenix, Ariz.
Website: vision54.com
Teaching since: 1982
Top 100 since: 1996
1992 LPGA Teacher of the Year

RICK McCORD
Facility: McCord Golf Academy, Orange Lake C.C., Orlando, Fla.
Website: themccordgolfacademy.com
Teaching since: 1973
Top 100 since: 1996

MIKE McGETRICK
Facility: Colorado G.C., Parker, Colo.
Website: coloradogolfclub.com
Teaching since: 1983
Top 100 since: 1996
1999 PGA Teacher of the Year

JIM McLEAN
Facility: Jim McLean Golf School, Miami, Fla.
Website: jimmclean.com
Teaching since: 1975
Top 100 since: 1996
1994 PGA Teacher of the Year

BRIAN MOGG
Facility: Waldorf Astoria G.C., Orlando, Fla.
Website: moggperformance.com
Teaching since: 1992
Top 100 since: 2005

BILL MORETTI
Facility: Moretti Golf, Austin, Texas
Website: morettigolf.com
Teaching since: 1979
Top 100 since: 1996

JERRY MOULDS
Facility: Pumpkin Ridge G.C., North Plains, Ore.
Teaching since: 1970
Top 100 since: 1996

SCOTT MUNROE
Facility: Nantucket G.C., Siasconset, Mass.
Website: moneygolf.net
Teaching since: 1978
Top 100 since: 2009

JIM MURPHY
Facility: Jim Murphy Golf at Sugar Creek C.C., Sugar Land, Texas
Website: jimmurphygolf.com
Teaching since: 1984
Top 100 since: 2003

TOM NESS
Facility: Reunion G.C., Hoschton, Ga.
Website: affinitigolfacademy.com
Teaching since: 1972
Top 100 since: 2007

PIA NILSSON
Facility: Legacy Golf Resort, Phoenix, Ariz.
Website: vision54.com
Teaching since: 1987
Top 100 since: 2001

DAN PASQUARIELLO
Facility: Pebble Beach Golf Academy, Pebble Beach, Calif.
Website: pebblebeach.com
Teaching since: 1970
Top 100 since: 2007

TOM PATRI
Facility: Friar's Head G.C., Riverhead, N.Y.
Website: tompatri.com
Teaching since: 1981
Top 100 since: 2001

BRUCE PATTERSON
Facility: Butler National G.C., Oak Brook, Ill.
Teaching since: 1980
Top 100 since: 2005

DAVE PELZ
Facility: Pelz Golf, Austin, Texas
Website: pelzgolf.com
Teaching since: 1976
Top 100 since: 1996

MIKE PERPICH
Facility: RiverPines G.C., Johns Creek, Ga.
Website: mikeperpich.com
Teaching since: 1980
Top 100 since: 2001

GALE PETERSON
Facility: Sea Island Golf Learning Center, St. Simons Island, Ga.
Website: seaisland.com
Teaching since: 1978
Top 100 since: 1996
1996 LPGA Teacher of the Year

E.J. PFISTER
Facility: Oak Tree, Edmond, Okla.
Website: ejpfistergolf.com
Teaching since: 1986
Top 100 since: 2009

DAVE PHILLIPS
Facility: TPI, Oceanside, Calif.
Website: mytpi.com
Teaching since: 1989
Top 100 since: 2001

CAROL PREISINGER
Facility: The Kiawah Island Club, Kiawah Island, S.C.
Website: carolpreisinger.com
Teaching since: 1986
Top 100 since: 2005

KIP PUTERBAUGH
Facility: The Aviara Golf Academy, Carlsbad, Calif.
Website: aviaragolfacademy.com
Teaching since: 1972
Top 100 since: 1996

NANCY QUARCELINO
Facility: Kings Creek G.C., Spring Hill, Tenn.
Website: qsog.com
Teaching since: 1979
Top 100 since: 2003
2000 LPGA Teacher of the Year

CARL RABITO
Facility: Bolingbrook G.C., Bolingbrook, Ill.
Website: rabitogolf.com
Teaching since: 1987
Top 100 since: 2007

DANA RADER
Facility: Ballantyne Resort, Charlotte, N.C.
Website: danarader.com
Teaching since: 1980
Top 100 since: 1996
1990 LPGA Teacher of the Year

BRAD REDDING
Facility: The Resort Club at Grande Dunes, Myrtle Beach, S.C.
Website: grandedunes.com
Teaching since: 1984
Top 100 since: 2001

BRADY RIGGS
Facility: Woodley Lakes G.C., Van Nuys, Calif.
Website: bradyriggs.com
Teaching since: 1990
Top 100 since: 2007

PHIL RITSON
Facility: Orange County National, Orlando, Fla.
Website: ocngolf.com
Teaching since: 1950
Top 100 since: 1996

SCOTT SACKETT
Facility: Scott Sackett Golf, Scottsdale, Ariz.
Website: scottsackett.com
Teaching since: 1985
Top 100 since: 1999

ADAM SCHRIBER
Facility: Crystal Mountain Resort, Thompsonville, Mich.
Website: crystalmountain.com
Teaching since: 1985
Top 100 since: 2009

CRAIG SHANKLAND
Facility: LPGA International, Daytona Beach, Fla.
Teaching since: 1957
Top 100 since: 1996
2001 PGA Teacher of the Year

MIKE SHANNON
Facility: Sea Island Golf Learning Center, St. Simons Island, Ga.
Website: seaisland.com
Teaching since: 1975
Top 100 since: 1996

TED SHEFTIC
Facility: Bridges G.C., Abbottstown, Pa.
Website: tedsheftic.com
Teaching since: 1966
Top 100 since: 2003

LAIRD SMALL
Facility: Pebble Beach Golf Academy, Pebble Beach, Calif.
Website: pebblebeach.com
Teaching since: 1979
Top 100 since: 1996
2003 PGA Teacher of the Year

RANDY SMITH
Facility: Royal Oaks C.C., Dallas, Texas
Teaching since: 1973
Top 100 since: 2001
2002 PGA Teacher of the Year

RICK SMITH
Facility: Treetops Resort, Gaylord, Mich.
Website: ricksmith.com
Teaching since: 1977
Top 100 since: 1996

TODD SONES
Facility: Impact Golf Schools at White Deer Run G.C., Vernon Hills, Ill.
Website: toddsones.com
Teaching since: 1982
Top 100 since: 1996

CHARLES SORRELL
Facility: Crystal Lake C.C., Hampton, Ga.
Website: sorrellgolf.com
Teaching since: 1966
Top 100 since: 1996
1990 PGA Teacher of the Year

MITCHELL SPEARMAN
Facility: Doral Arrowwood Golf Resort, Rye Brook, N.Y.
Website: mitchellspearman.com
Teaching since: 1979
Top 100 since: 1996

MARK STEINBAUER
Facility: Carlton Woods, The Woodlands, Texas
Website: thewoodlands.com
Teaching since: 1977
Top 100 since: 2011

KELLIE STENZEL
Facility: Palm Beach G.C., Palm Beach, Fla.
Website: kelliestenzelgolf.com
Teaching since: 1990
Top 100 since: 2009

TOM STICKNEY
Facility: Bighorn G.C., Palm Desert, Calif.
Website: tomstickneygolf.com
Teaching since: 1990
Top 100 since: 2007

DR. JIM SUTTIE
Facility: Cog Hill G.C., Lemont, Ill.; TwinEagles, Naples, Fla.
Website: jimsuttie.com
Teaching since: 1972
Top 100 since: 1996
2000 PGA Teacher of the Year

JON TATTERSALL
Facility: Terminus Club, Atlanta, Ga.
Website: terminusclub.com
Teaching since: 1988
Top 100 since: 2007

DR. T.J. TOMASI
Facility: Tomasi Golf, Port St. Lucie, Fla.
Website: tjtomasi.com
Teaching since: 1975
Top 100 since: 1999

J.D. TURNER
Facility: The Landings, Savannah, Ga.
Website: jdturnergolf.com
Teaching since: 1965
Top 100 since: 1996

STAN UTLEY
Facility: Grayhawk Learning Center, Scottsdale, Ariz.
Website: stanutleygolf.com
Teaching since: 1986
Top 100 since: 2009

CHUCK WINSTEAD
Facility: The University Club, Baton Rouge, La.
Website: universityclubbr.com
Teaching since: 1993
Top 100 since: 2005

DR. DAVID WRIGHT
Facility: Wright Balance Golf Academy at Arroyo Trabuco G.C., Mission Viejo, Calif.
Website: wrightbalance.com
Teaching since: 1982
Top 100 since: 2005

Get more information on *Golf Magazine's* Top 100 Teachers in America, plus exclusive video lessons, tips and drills at

GOLF.com

WORLD GOLF TEACHERS HALL OF FAME
The master class of the Top 100 Teachers in America

PEGGY KIRK BELL
Facility: Pine Needles Resort, Southern Pines, N.C.
Teaching since: 1958
Top 100/Hall of Fame since: 1996/1998
1961 LPGA Teacher of the Year

MANUEL De La TORRE
Facility: Milwaukee C.C., River Hills, Wis.
Website: manueldelatorregolf.com
Teaching since: 1948
Top 100/Hall of Fame since: 1996/1998
1986 PGA Teacher of the Year

JIM FLICK
Facility: TaylorMade Performance Lab, Carlsbad, Calif.
Website: jimflick.com
Teaching since: 1954
Top 100/Hall of Fame since: 1996/2002
1988 PGA Teacher of the Year

DAVID LEADBETTER
Facility: David Leadbetter Golf Academy, Champions Gate, Fla.
Website: davidleadbetter.com
Teaching since: 1976
Top 100/Hall of Fame since: 1996/2007

EDDIE MERRINS
Facility: Bel-Air C.C., Los Angeles, Calif.
Website: eddiemerrins.com
Teaching since: 1957
Top 100/Hall of Fame since: 1996/2008

BOB TOSKI
Facility: Toski-Battersby Learning Center, Coconut Creek, Fla.
Website: learn-golf.com
Teaching since: 1956
Top 100/Hall of Fame since: 1996/1999

DR. GARY WIREN
Facility: Trump International, West Palm Beach, Fla.
Website: garywiren.com
Teaching since: 1955
Top 100/Hall of Fame since: 1996/2007
1987 PGA Teacher of the Year

GOLF MAGAZINE

EDITOR
David M. Clarke

CREATIVE DIRECTOR
Paul Crawford

EXECUTIVE EDITOR
Eamon Lynch

ART DIRECTOR
Paul Ewen

MANAGING EDITORS
David DeNunzio (Instruction)
Gary Perkinson (Production)
Robert Sauerhaft (Equipment)

EDITOR AT LARGE
Connell Barrett

DEPUTY MANAGING EDITOR
Michael Chwasky (Instruction & Equipment)

SENIOR EDITORS
Alan Bastable, Michael Walker, Jr.,
Joseph Passov (Travel/Course Rankings)

**SENIOR EDITOR, GOLF MAGAZINE
CUSTOM PUBLISHING**
Thomas Mackin

DEPUTY ART DIRECTOR
Karen Ha

PHOTO EDITOR
Carrie Boretz

SENIOR WRITERS
Michael Bamberger, Damon Hack, Cameron
Morfit, Alan Shipnuck, Gary Van Sickle

ASSOCIATE EDITOR
Steven Beslow

ASSISTANT EDITOR
Jessica Marksbury

PUBLISHER
Dick Raskopf

DIRECTOR OF BUSINESS DEVELOPMENT
Brad J. Felenstein

SPECIAL THANKS
Michael Adams, Christine Austin, Katherine Barnet,
Virgil Bastos, Jeremy Biloon, Rose Cirrincione,
Lauren Hall Clark, Caroline DeNunzio, Davey DeNunzio,
Dominick DeNunzio, Harvey Ewen, Jacqueline Fitzgerald,
Christine Font, Jenna Goldberg, Karen Ha, Hillary Hirsch,
Suzanne Janso, David Kahn, Amy Mangus,
Robert Marasco, Kimberly Marshall, Amy Migliaccio,
Nina Mistry, Dave Rozzelle, Carmel Sweeney,
Adriana Tierno, Time Inc. Studios,
Dr. T.J. Tomasi, Vanessa Wu

Sports Illustrated

EDITOR, TIME INC. SPORTS GROUP
Terry McDonell

MANAGING EDITOR, SI.com
Paul Fichtenbaum

MANAGING EDITOR, SI GOLF GROUP
James P. Herre

PRESIDENT, TIME INC. SPORTS GROUP
Mark Ford

V.P., PUBLISHER
Frank Wall

SENIOR V.P., CONSUMER MARKETING
Nate Simmons

V.P., COMMUNICATIONS AND DEVELOPMENT
Scott Novak

ASSOC. PUBLISHER, MKTG. AND CREATIVE SERVICES
Charlie Saunders

SENIOR V.P., FINANCE
Elissa Fishman

V.P., FINANCE
Peter Greer

VICE PRESIDENT
Ann Marie Doherty

V.P., OPERATIONS
Brooke Twyford

LEGAL
Judith Margolin

HUMAN RESOURCES DIRECTOR
Liz Matilla

GOLF MAGAZINE'S BIG BOOK OF BASICS
by *Golf Magazine's* Basics Team

EDITOR
David DeNunzio

ART DIRECTION/BOOK DESIGN
Paul Ewen

PHOTOGRAPHY
Angus Murray, Schecter Lee (Ch. 5)

ILLUSTRATIONS
Robin Griggs (1957–2008)

IMAGING
Geoffrey A. Michaud (Director, *SI* Imaging)
Dan Larkin, Robert M. Thompson,
Gerald Burke, Neil Clayton

COPY EDITORS
Don Armstrong, Joseph Mills

EDITORIAL CONSULTANTS
Dave Allen, Michael Chwasky

A SPORTS ILLUSTRATED PUBLICATION

Time HOME ENTERTAINMENT

PUBLISHER
Jim Childs

**VICE PRESIDENT,
BUSINESS DEVELOPMENT & STRATEGY**
Steven Sandonato

EXECUTIVE DIRECTOR, MARKETING SERVICES
Carol Pittard

EXECUTIVE DIRECTOR, RETAIL & SPECIAL SALES
Tom Mifsud

EXECUTIVE PUBLISHING DIRECTOR
Joy Butts

DIRECTOR, BOOKAZINE DEVELOPMENT & MARKETING
Laura Adam

FINANCE DIRECTOR
Glenn Buonocore

ASSOCIATE PUBLISHING DIRECTOR
Megan Pearlman

ASSISTANT GENERAL COUNSEL
Helen Wan

ASSISTANT DIRECTOR, SPECIAL SALES
Ilene Schreider

SENIOR BOOK PRODUCTION MANAGER
Susan Chodakiewicz

DESIGN & PREPRESS MANAGER
Anne-Michelle Gallero

ASSOCIATE PREPRESS MANAGER
Alex Voznesenskiy

ASSISTANT BRAND MANAGER
Stephanie Braga

EDITORIAL DIRECTOR
Stephen Koepp

EDITORIAL OPERATIONS DIRECTOR
Michael Q. Bullerdick

GOLF.com

EXECUTIVE EDITOR
Charlie Hanger

EXECUTIVE PRODUCER
Christopher Shade

DEPUTY EDITOR
David Dusek

SENIOR PRODUCERS
Ryan Reiterman, Jeff Ritter

ASSOCIATE PRODUCER
Kevin Cunningham